Weddings:

The Good, the Bad, and the Scary

by Darlene J. Forbes

DORRANCE
PUBLISHING CO
EST. 1920
PITTSBURGH, PENNSYLVANIA 15238

Dorrance Publishing Co
585 Alpha Drive
Suite 103
Pittsburgh, PA 15238
Visit our website at *www.dorrancebookstore.com*

ISBN: 978-1-6366-1270-6
eISBN: 978-1-6366-1856-2

Photos provided by

Ken Viale
Richard Wood
Dan Jeffers

Dedication to:

My family Debbie, Kim, Rhonda and Jim,

Thanks for your support in this incredible journey

Weddings:

The Good, the Bad, and the Scary

Chapter 1:

How it All Started

IT WAS 1980-SOMETHING WHEN I HAD THE BRILLIANT IDEA to start this business. We were on a fishing trip with friends when I was asked what I had done for fun the previous Saturday night. I had actually been at a friend's wedding, which was becoming more frequent. I have three daughters and it seemed that one of the girls was in a wedding as a flower girl, junior bridesmaid, or at least a guest. So I was frequently asked to cut the cake, make the punch, loan a tablecloth; I was basically free labor.

My fishing friend from the Big Apple told me that in New York, wedding planning and coordinating is a big business and I should give it a try. I should mention that I live in Napa, California, a small town in the wine country. Now we're very famous for wineries and tourism. Then we were popular for prunes, agriculture, and our local mental hospital. Most of the kids of my generation picked prunes in the summer to pay for school clothes or for spending money. Nowadays our teenagers wouldn't consider this menial job, sporting smashed prunes on their jeans.

I grew up a third generation Napan in a simpler time. We were a normal family of the 1950s: black and white TV, one car in the garage, and a once a year vacation consisting of camping and fishing. My father worked in the local naval shipyard, and my mother was a stay at home housewife/artist. I had an older sister who thought I was a pest, which I'm sure

1

I was. My dad lived to fish and hunt on the weekends, and my mother spent her afternoons painting and drawing in the dining room.

Mom's artwork was the 1930s Betty Boop style, risqué but fun. I still have some of Mom's early sketches. As I child I enjoyed bluebirds, camp-fire girls, dance lessons, and a very brief stint with a violin, which I had to give up when I sat on it.

As an adult, during the week, Monday through Friday, I worked as an accountant, first in manufacturing and then later for a construction and trucking company. It was a learning and challenging experience often deal-ing with construction workers, trying to get these guys to turn in their hours for payroll or records for the PUC. More than once I had to climb on a chair look these guys in the eye and demand their paperwork. "If you want to get paid, give me your paperwork now, dammit."

Soon I was known to the drivers as Dammit Darlene. I think this work experience toughened me up for the future brides and grooms to come. I also use the word "dammit" more than I probably should have.

My mother was my steady babysitter for my workweek and also for the occasional wedding on the weekends. Sadly, we lost her in a house fire when my youngest daughter was eleven. My father had died years before at the age of sixty-one of lung cancer, possibly associated with his years working in a shipyard. Now, no longer having a babysitter, I depended on my two teenage daughters, and I often took my youngest to the weddings where she hung out with the catering staff and learned to appreciate ex-cellent food.

This new challenge in the wedding industry could be a good hobby and very profitable if I handled it right. Life had been fairly mundane up until this point. I worked, took my girls to baseball practice, cheerleading, and skating lessons, and donated the balance of my off time to the PTA and the occasional camping trip with my family. So yes, I was ready for a new adventure. While driving to all these activities, I had time to ponder the possibilities. I am known for being a slow, conservative driver, so when I'm pondering, I can actually be considered a slow driver or better known to my daughters as "The Turtle."

One evening, I was driving with the girls to Sacramento for my youngest daughter's skating lesson. Driving along in the slow lane, enjoying the nice evening, I noticed passing cars honking and people in the cars laughing and pointing at my car. I know I'm slow and yes, cautious, but I'm not that slow. I asked, "What are these people honking at?" The girls were giggling in the back seat, but that's not unusual. When we arrived at the rink in Sacramento, I got out of the car to open the trunk. "Oh, now I get it." On the back of my car bumper was a very nicely printed sign: "Beware: Driver on Valium." I knew the culprit had to be my oldest, Debbie, a serious prankster. I tried to explain the seriousness of this issue and what if I'd been stopped by the highway patrol? Really!

From what I knew there were no wedding coordinators or event planners in Napa at this time. No one even knew what that was or what that entailed. Hell, I didn't know what it entailed. Today you can take classes, attend seminars, and obtain a license to become an event planner. In the eighties, it sounded like a made up job. I had no experience, no training, but I would figure it out as I went. Maybe if I knew now what I didn't know then, I might have chickened out. I was to learn that it's more important to know what not to do at a wedding than what to do. It takes a strong constitution, thick skin, and good arches. This business will ruin your tootsies.

I had lots to think about this new concept, this wedding planning business. I could be the first planner in our little valley. Where would my clients come from? How do I begin? Well, I'm sure there must be a bride out there that knew less than I did. So, several weeks later on my lunch break, I went to city hall and applied for a business license. By using my own name, I didn't need to get a fictitious name. With a little imagination I designed an inexpensive business card, made up a few flyers, and I was ready to go, right? There were no books on this topic in those early days so I would go on my intuition and common sense. I also needed advice from people actually in the wedding business.

The following Saturday, I decided to visit wedding vendors, photographers, florists, musicians, bakeries, and stationary stores that print invitations. All these vendors have contacts with brides-to-be. Once I explained my objectives, most agreed to assist in my endeavors if I would help them get more business. "How can I do this when I don't know what I'm doing?" Well, as one very kind woman who owned the local stationary store mentioned, we should hold a bridal faire to reach out to future brides. She had read about these shows in wedding magazines.

I started looking for venues to hold this event. Napa had few hotels at that time, maybe three or four, and most weddings were held at hotels, country clubs, or the local fairgrounds.

Our most famous motel, the Casa Lu Al, had the distinction of having had Elvis Presley stay there in 1961 while filming the movie *Wild in the Country* with Tuesday Weld. My mother used to take us by there to sneak a peek of Elvis. But I am regressing back to those exciting days of my youth.

Most wineries at that point could not hold weddings. Even now, there are very few in our county that can hold a wedding. The county must issue permits to allow wineries to host a wedding. My last hotel to visit on my Saturday rounds was our local Clarion Hotel, and they agreed to host this event, offer a champagne welcome, and provide the ballroom, tables, and linens for this bridal faire. . I was thrilled! Wow, I did it. Now I had to find the vendors, pick a date, and figure out how to advertise and promote this endeavor.

I reached out to a florist I had known for years and then a photographer, DJ, stationary store, and a minister, and when I was finished, I had twenty wedding related vendors, one professional in each category. Next step, pick a date, set up a group meeting, and plan advertising. We agreed if everyone paid a small amount, I believe it was three hundred dollars, that would pay for advertising, flyers, newspaper, etc. At that time, there was no social media, so advertising had to be done by newspaper ads and flyers. At one of first vendor meetings we picked a date, a Sunday afternoon between three and six o'clock. That way couples are home and more likely to attend. Free booze and appetizers—why not stop by?

I should mention my husband and daughters thought I was nuts, but they decided the best way to handle me was just let me go. I would give up and run out of steam eventually. However, if someone says I can't do something, it just makes me more determined. I was kind of like a pimple on the nose; if you ignore it, it will go away.

Back to business: I contacted the local newspaper, worked with a very kind lady, and put together an advertising schedule that the group could afford. We named our team the Wine Country Wedding Association. It has a nice ring to it, don't you agree? Flyers were printed and put up in store windows all over town. Or at least in stores that would let me. Our date was scheduled for a Sunday in January. It makes sense since couples often get engaged over the Christmas holidays.

As we got closer, I was either energized or terrified. I was spending most weekends and evenings working on this project. I couldn't let these trusting vendors down, and I didn't want to tarnish my own reputation, which by the way, I had not yet established. I had yet to do a wedding or have a client. I was hoping this faire would bring me some trusting brides.

The week before the show, I picked up brochures at the printers, went over details with the hotel, and prayed. We had no idea how many brides would show. We had asked each vendor to give a small gift to raffle off, and one of our vendors a travel agent was offering a free trip for two to Hawaii, air included. This, I hoped, would be our big draw. Wanting to look my best, I decided to have my hair frosted with blond streaks. I had very dark brown hair at the time, so I thought a few blond streaks would give me a sophisticated professional look. Well, my hairdresser was not comfortable with this, so I asked a friend who had some experience, so she said, and she offered to do the deed. As it turned out I ended up with a bright red large streak in the front of my head. Apparently she didn't leave the bleach on long enough or just didn't know what she was doing. So here I was, looking like Woody Woodpecker. I had planned to wear a new red dress for the evening, but now I couldn't because my hair clashed with my dress and gave my face had an orange tint.

Sunday came, and we had a great turnout. More than two hundred and fifty brides came, some with moms, some with best friends. Wow, total surprise! I'm sure some just came for the free liquor, but still, we had people. I was so busy running the check in and welcoming brides that I didn't even think about manning my own booth. I had set up a nice flower arrangement, a bottle of champagne that would be my raffle gift, and some business cards. I had no pictures of weddings to show, because I hadn't done any weddings yet. Well, they would come. The vendors were very grateful and promised to refer me. We did this show for twenty-five years once a year, same vendors, various locations. These vendors are still my friends and recommended by me to this day.

Chapter 2:

My First Wedding

I'M NOT SURE HOW I GOT MY FIRST BRIDE, possibly through the show or the ads, but I had a live one. Both the bride and groom were wonderful, kind, and very easy to work with. I didn't tell them they were my first victims, um, wedding, but just put on my best face of "fake it till you make it" routine. This was approximately four months after the show. I also had no idea of how much to charge. I thought of a percentage of the wedding cost, or a flat fee, and finally decided on a flat fee. I wanted to get more business and keep my price reasonable. I was told several years later by a client that I don't charge enough. I probably still don't but I want to be available for all brides in all price ranges, and I just enjoy what I do.

The wedding was six months away at a country club in the upper valley, smack in the middle of the wine country. The wedding was now what I term "full service," where I located most of the vendors. The wedding was to be midsized, seventy-five to one hundred guests, simple and elegant. The venue would provide the meal and bar service, all other vendors would need to be hired. The bride wanted a piano for the live music for the ceremony and cocktail hour and a DJ for dinner and dancing. I located a lady who literally had a business "Have piano, will travel," and she was hired. The only problem was that she brought her real piano, not a keyboard. She brought her piano up in the back of a pickup truck; the ceremony itself was located up a hill with a road too narrow to drive up. I finally found two gentlemen that worked at the venue and they hooked up a pulley system and rope to pull this piano on wheels up the hill. Thank God, the piano, the pianist, and I got there early. First crisis averted. The rest of the wedding and day went by without problems or issues. I cried at the ceremony with relief, pride, and joy for the couple. I was flying by the seat of my pants, one wedding down, hopefully more to go. Our couple was very happy and six months later asked me to plan and cater a Christmas house warming party for them. But that's another story under my catering career.

I did get more weddings after that, but not many. The valley had not yet become a destination for weddings. That would come some fifteen years later. Most of my weddings at that time were local brides, held at local hotels, country clubs, and fairgrounds. I continued to work as an accountant during the week and do the occasional wedding during the weekend.

Chapter 3:

The Early Years

I REMEMBER ONE WEDDING I DID AT THE FAIRGROUNDS. It was an evening wedding with approximately one hundred and fifty guests. The bride's mother had hired me and was very much in charge. We had a live band, local caterer, florist, etc.

All was going well and the dancing had started. One of the guests came over to me and mentioned that a guest, a woman, was ill and not speaking. I went over to her, and she was slumped down and appeared to be unconscious. I asked her tablemates if she had been drinking too much, but her companions said no, it was the overheated room. I went to the bride's mother and mentioned that I wanted to get the guest outside and possibly call 911. The mother went ballistic and said, "Absolutely not! She's not going to ruin my daughter's wedding," I went back to the guest and tried to awaken her myself. That didn't work, and she was not really aware of her environment. Finally the band leader noticed my attempts to pick up someone larger than I am; literally a dead weight. He came to my aid and helped me take her outside to a bench. The bride's mother was hot on our tail. Mom was screaming at him to get the music going again and for me to deal with this unconscious woman. Well, thank God, the band leader told the irate mother that if I was not allowed to call for help, he was not going to play another song. That did it, and I called 911 and stayed with her until the ambulance came. She was starting to revive a bit by the time the ambulance arrived. They did transport her, and I never did hear how it ended. The bride's mother pretended nothing had happened, and I continued on with my duties, but I lost all respect for the bride's mother.

∞

I was learning more with each wedding, gaining confidence, but also knew I had a long way to go. Each wedding is different with new challenges. I did some weddings at private homes and low budgets. The family would provide the food and they just wanted someone to oversee getting the bride down the aisle. Some of these times, I would hire helpers to set up tables, put out food, replenish food, and clean up. I also found out that coordinating and planning can also mean lifting and moving tables and all sorts of heavy objects. You can also be treated as more of a servant than a professional. I had to learn to speak up and outline my duties and responsibilities—not sure I ever got the point across.

In the early days I kept a file and notes for each bride but not the detailed timelines that I now use and have used for the past fifteen years or so. Now each timeline is approximately five pages long with details as to all vendors, names, numbers, and timing of all events during the day as to the wedding, cocktail hour, dinner, dancing, toasts, etc. All vendors now receive a copy of the timeline so that we're all on the same page. It's also easier now with email and text capabilities. In the old days all had to be done by phone calls. The timing of a wedding is crucial, and a wedding is a team effort. Every vendor is a member of that team, and all need to be on the same page. A wedding can go smoothly because of a great team or turn into a disaster because of one or two vendors that want to beat their own drum. Hiring the right professional is so important. Get references, talk to other vendors, and find out who does and does not work well together.

I have had many experiences of working with family members that want to provide the food, cake, flowers, photograph the wedding, etc. As

I tell my brides that may be thinking of using a family member or friend, make sure that they are willing to work with our timing and guidelines. I need to be able to talk to the vendor that has been hired or offered their services, that if the flowers, cake, etc. are not satisfactory, I need to know that they will correct that product and have time to make that correction. I can't call out or tell your family member that the cake is awful, the flowers wilted, and their loving work is icky. I do recommend hiring a professional rather than imposing on a friend or family member to save money or perhaps honor them by asking them to provide a service. I have many stories of these wonderful surprises by family members.

I should probably throw in at some point that I did end up getting divorced. I don't think the weddings and my crazy business had anything to do with this, but after eighteen years, it just didn't work anymore. We did remain friends, at least until he passed. So here I am, a single mother, accountant, and a part time wedding planner trying to support her daughters. This brings us to my next professional endeavor: business number two to provide additional support for us.

Chapter 4:

Catering, or Darlene Cooks

As I MENTIONED EARLIER, MY FIRST BRIDE asked me to help plan and cater an open house Christmas party. I have always loved to cook, so yes, I can and would do this. You will also hear this statement again: I seem to believe in the Little Engine that could, "I think I can, I think I can." This has always been my motto and I raised my daughters to believe you can do anything, if you want it badly enough. Oh, and if what you want is legal. You just have to want it enough. Sometimes our engines chug more than normal, especially uphill, but who has a perfect engine?

I began to work on a simple menu: fondue, meatballs in a whiskey sauce, quiche, and mini sandwiches with chocolates for dessert. The couple provided the bar and I provided the food and the staffing. The staffing provided by my daughters, Debbie, Kim, and Rhonda, wearing all black and Santa hats. I can't say they were thrilled, but I was paying them, so they did show up. The open house was scheduled from six to eight in the evening, just drinks and appetizers. All went well, and the food and drinks were good; all in all, maybe too good. Eight o'clock came, then nine, then ten, and no one was leaving. They just kept eating and drinking.

The food was getting low, and my girls were getting upset. "Mom, when are we leaving? You're not getting paid to stay this late, and I want overtime pay." One gentleman literally stood over the fondue pot, stuffed

his face, and then asked me for the recipe. He also offered his opinion that it needed a bit more wine.

Finally at half past ten, I told our hostess that we were finished and that I would come back the next day and pick up my pots, pans, and trays. I went back the next day and the fondue pot had been broken, but the hostess did offer to replace it. I was learning early on that you need to set boundaries. I had charged one amount for the food, time, and the whole evening. When we stayed over time, I lost money if I paid the girls their full wages, which of course, I had to if I wanted to use their services again.

Other catering jobs just seemed to come along. Most came with weddings, but not all. One of my couples had a fairgrounds wedding with a tight budget, so somehow I offered to cater, with a reasonable charge. The guest count was over four hundred people, so my catering was not what you call fine dining. It consisted of deli trays, pans of pasta, quiche, large green salads, rolls, and basic side dishes. These were dishes that I could prep at home and cook or reheat on site. Salads could be made and mixed in large new garbage bags and then put in bowls and topped with dressing just before the meal service. I used the kitchen on site to heat the pasta dishes and the rest of the set up. A very kind local grocery store let me use their walk in freezers to store these twenty to twenty-five pans of pasta until the day of the wedding. I bought large quantities of pasta, quiche, and rolls at Costco and other wholesale outlets. For staff I hired high school kids and friends of my daughters. I provided the burgundy aprons and bow ties and they wore all black. They were grateful for the money and I was grateful for the help. I usually did buffets, much easier for large crowds. With two or three of the kids in the kitchen mixing the salads and heating the pastas, three or four out front refilling the buffet table, and three or four pulling the trays and cleaning in the kitchen, we had it down to a science.

The bride provided the china or paper plates and linens; we provided the food, serving dishes, and trays. I would be at the wedding, normally at a church, get the bride down the aisle, then run back to the reception area to meet the kids and finish setting up to feed the guests. Add a touch of red wine to frozen pasta, and wow, it tastes like homemade. I would change clothes quickly and be ready to roll. These were crazy times, but so fun. The kids were great. I still see some of them today, and I'm sure they have great stories to share with their children.

One of my male helpers got married a few years ago, and I was very proud to be his coordinator. Oh, and by the way, he turned out be a very famous Broadway producer in New York. He and his brother both worked for me. I'm very proud of all these wonderful young people. Most of these kids were band members and continued on to college and great careers.

Catering is grueling work, and in the beginning, I lost money. I did not take into account the hours to clean up after the event and leave the venue spotless. Dishes to be done, counters and ovens to clean, and floors to mop. I would quote a price for food and staffing and allow time, but obviously not enough time. The caterers I now work with have my heartfelt respect. It's back breaking work; setting up tables, dropping linens, carrying, serv-ing, and cleaning, oh my! The hours are long, and we would often still be cleaning up at midnight or later. My youngest daughter would often curl up on a table in the kitchen and sleep while I finished cleaning.

Friends and business don't always gel. I had taken a couple of college classes with a young man some fifteen years prior when he contacted me to possibly cater his wedding. We had been sort of friends and had gone out one date, but that really hadn't gelled either. He had seen my ad and gave me a phone call. I met with Jeff and his fiancée Mary, and we decided on a buffet menu and the pricing. The ceremony was in a church and the reception at a Moose or Elks hall. I don't remember exactly which it was, but it was a nice hall and they provided the tables, linens, chairs, china, etc. so all I had to provide was the food and use their small but tidy kitchen.

The evening went well and the food was enjoyed by all. My girls were clearing the buffet and cleaning the kitchen when the dancing started. After the first dance with the bride and groom, the other guests joined in. The groom came over and asked me to dance. I told him that I don't normally dance at events that I was working, but thank you for asking. He insisted, so yes, I gave in and danced. My girls came out of the kitchen to watch and giggle. I might add that I am a very good dancer, so there was no need for them to be embarrassed.

When the dance was over I went back to work in the kitchen when I was surprised by three women friends of the bride. They wanted to let me know that the bride was upset and in tears in the bathroom because I had danced with the groom. She did not know we had dated and "how could I do this to her at her wedding?" What, you are kidding me? What in the hell had he told his bride? One date, friends, and this comes down to tears and accusations? I finished up the kitchen, loaded my van, and sought out the groom. "Do you know your bride is upset and believes that you and I have or had a relationship?" He was very calm and told me that she's just emotional, had too much to drink, and not to let it bother me. Oh no, don't let it bother me; I was getting glares from every woman in the room.

I could read their minds: *bitch, home wrecker, wild catering hoe.* You get the picture. We quickly finished loading and got the hell out of Dodge. I did read in the vital statistic some years later that they had gotten divorced. Thank God, I didn't hear from Jeff again.

I do remember a couple of near disasters, but by the grace of God and good luck we pulled them off. In one of our busiest years, we seemed to book a large percentage of these in a town over on the Sonoma Coast. I guess word travels fast that I'm either very good or very cheap. I suspect the latter.

One specific event was for an outdoor wedding at a beautiful state park close to the beach. I met with the bride, picked the menu, and named a price for the one hundred and fifty guest count. I then drove to the coast to look at the site. Very rustic, lots of trees, and the kitchen was literally an open air shack with a roof and open on all four sides. However the so-called kitchen did have a sink, stove, oven, refrigerator, and a table in the center. There was also a large open pit with firewood and a grill. So, yes, I could make this work.

Dining tables were wooden tables and benches, so no linens to put in place. The buffet would be set up on a large wooden table in the center of the dining tables. A bartending service had been hired by the bride, so I didn't have to worry about drinks or glassware, just the food.

The day of the wedding, my team and I (my fifteen-year-old daughter Rhonda and two of her fifteen- year-old girlfriends, who were frequently part of my staff) showed up at this rustic venue just as the fog was lifting. We arrived early and set to work unloading the food and wiping down the work surfaces. The bride had chosen chicken breasts to be grilled with pasta, rolls, and various salads. I turned on the oven to start heating the chicken and then all I would need is to place it on the grill with a light sauce, and the pasta could heat in the oven.

Well, guess what? Neither the oven nor the stove was working. What the hell! I had the phone number of the local park ranger and I gave him a call. To his credit, he was there in ten minutes. I told him my problem and he said, "Well, I guess it's not working, but nothing I can do about it today." Now I am getting upset. My bride paid for this facility. She was told it was a working kitchen, and I have three hundred frozen chicken breasts to cook.

I took a deep breath to steady myself then said, "Okay, sir, we have a serious situation here. Where do you live and do you have a kitchen?"

"Well, yes," he said, "my wife and I live down the road apiece, and I guess you can use my kitchen."

I left two of the girls at the site to continue with set up, and my daughter and I followed him to his home. We explained to his very nice, elderly wife that we were going to use their oven. I really didn't give them a choice. I left my daughter for two hours to cook pan after pan of chicken breasts. She was not a happy camper and couldn't believe I would leave her with two virtual strangers that could be killers.

"Really, kiddo, he's a park ranger, and he must have a badge somewhere. He looks honorable, so start cooking." I headed back to the wilderness kitchen. The girls and I proceeded to light the open fire pit to heat pan after pan of pasta. Once heated, we would wrap them in foil to stay warm. We finished all of our set up, and I drove back to pick up my daughter and the chicken.

Just as we finished setting up our makeshift buffet table, the bridal party and the guests starting arriving. The ceremony was very simple. It was held between two large trees and the guests stood for the fifteen-minute ceremony. After the ceremony the couple took off with the photographers to get ocean view shots. To our good fortune, the cocktail hour continued for one and a half hours while the couple continued with the photos. That gave us time to put the chicken and pasta back on the grill. I added more cheese and wine to the pasta to keep it moist over this unmonitored heat, and extra sauce to the chicken. We just kept alternating trays of chicken and pasta over the open flames. The pasta burned a little on the bottom, but there wasn't much we could do but add a touch more wine and cheese to cover the scorched noodles.

Finally our couple returned, the guests were well oiled, and the buffet was set up, and we prayed. Everyone loved the food, and the bride and groom couldn't have been happier. I think the amount of alcohol may have had something to do with it. We started clean up and the dancing began.

Once the guests were leaving and it was getting dark (no outside lighting), we started to pack up my van. The girls had been amazing and were very proud of themselves, as was I. When we were ready to drive off, I noticed that Jen, one of my girls, was missing. Where did she go? Then we heard some yelling in the distance and we followed the voice. We found

Jen locked in an outhouse. The door was stuck. She had been stuck in there for ten minutes, and the smell was not pleasant. However, the day ended well, and the bride referred me for other weddings in that area.

Lesson learned: always check out the venue well before the event and make sure everything is working as promised. Bathroom deodorizer was also added to my catering kit.

Another catering venture that turned interesting was at a private estate poolside. I had gone to school with the bride's mother, so they hired me to coordinate and cater. For this wedding I brought in my staff and bartenders and rented the tables, chairs, linens, china, and glassware. The ceremony went off without a hitch. We were set up for dinner, and the cocktail hour was in full swing. Suddenly I heard a commotion around the pool and we saw first the bride and then the groom jump into the pool with their wedding clothes on. Next in were both sets of parents and a few other guests. Yes, it was a hot day, but what about the bride's dress and the groom's rented tuxedo? I bet he would get charged for that. I heard one of my staff shout to me and as I looked around, the bride's dad starting running toward me, picked me up, and jumped into the pool with me with my shoes still on. You might say I was not happy, but the person paying you is always right. I spent the rest of the day in a ruined dress, soggy shoes, and looking like a drowned rat. The bride and groom went into the house to change. I, however, did not have that luxury.

My staff said they would walk off the job it anyone tried to throw them in. Thank God no one bothered them. The rest of the day went off great with eating, drinking, and swimming.

We did do another catering job for a fifty-something guest wedding at a state park in Sonoma County.

I met with the couple who were very into nature and wanted an outdoor morning ceremony as the sun was coming up. I met with this couple and the venue a month or so before the wedding to pick out the menu. This was, again, rustic with no power source, so the menu had to be mostly cold foods or served at room temperature. The food also had to be hauled in three-quarters of a mile by hand, no road access.

There was a small picnic area in the middle of this rustic setting, and I would set those tables up with cloth linens and napkins, but I would use nice paper plates and utensils. The menu had to be simple but sustaining. We chose fruit trays, quiche at room temperature, cold salmon, fresh pastries, and banana cupcakes for dessert. Drinks were iced coffee, iced tea, orange juice, mimosas, and Bloody Marys for those that wanted or needed an eye opener. Coffee would have been nice, but I couldn't find an extension cord that would stretch a mile.

I arrived early, just as the sun was starting to come up, which would give me an hour or so before the guests arrived. We set out the linens and a separate table for the buffet. My staff was my middle daughter, Kim, youngest daughter, Rhonda, and our teenage band friend, Jen. By the time we hauled in all this food and ice, we were already exhausted. I also noticed something that I had not seen before on my previous visit: signs reading, BEWARE OF RATTLE SNAKES. Just so you know I am terrified of snakes, so I was not comfortable with this site. When had these signs gone up? Was this snake season? Is there a snake season?

When our couple arrived with their minister and guests, I pulled the groom aside and showed him one of the numerous snake signs. "Should we warn your guests?" I asked.

My groom responded with, "This may make my guests nervous, please cover the signs. I don't want them to worry." The bride and groom were both doctors and felt they had the situation in hand. What, did they have snakebite anti-venom in their car? Was this normal for this outdoorsy couple? I quickly covered all the snake signs with cloth napkins and then prayed. The ceremony went well, brunch was inhaled, and when we left the guests were happily finishing off the balance of the booze. We loaded out the dirty trays and dishes while keeping our eyes glued to the ground. We got out faster than we got in. I did get a thank you note a few weeks later, so apparently no one got bit. Another reminder to me: check out future locations for power, snakes, and other wild creatures.

The catering did continue and it allowed me extra money to keep my family going. We did Bar Mitzvahs, birthday parties, graduations, even a bank opening. We were gaining experience, improving our menu, and becoming more time efficient. I created new salad recipes and ventured into fancier meals. I did learn short cuts, and instead of buying prepared meat and cheese trays, I made my own with the help of a professional meat slicer loaned by a friend. I had a dear neighbor who lost his wife, and he would come over after work on Friday nights to slice meat, cut fruit, and help load my car. I think he also ate much of my profits. But again, catering and weddings are a team effort.

Chapter 5:

Balloons and Décor

IN THE EARLY NINETIES, BALLOONS were becoming popular in décor. I began noticing that balloon hearts and arches were being featured in many magazines. They were being used for parties, weddings, graduations, and the like. I thought, *okay, I can do this*. I can use them for décor for weddings and maybe parties. I decided to experiment. Balloon arches need helium, but the hearts and shaped structures need compressed air, not helium. One weekend I rented a small helium tank and a little air compressor. I needed to make a frame for the heart, but I wasn't sure how to do this. I went to Home Depot and bought four different kinds of wire. I bent the various wires into different shapes. The wires I first tried would not hold the shape, as they were too light. I continued until I found a wire that was strong enough to hold the shape but not so thick that I couldn't wrap balloons around it. I then pulled and pried the wires into a heart shape, and then joined them with heavy black tape. The frame had to be weighted down for a few days to stay in shape. I held them down with heavy books and encyclopedias. The living room floor was covered with frames stacked with books.

Next weekend, I did the same drill until I got it right. I ordered balloons from a catalog. I used either five or nine inches for the wire frames. For larger balloons, I used nine to eleven inches for the helium. I would use the air compressor to blow up the balloons, tie four together by using the stems, and then wrap around the frame. I tied four about every ten to twelve inches on the frame so no part of the frame is visible. Obviously some pop if you push too hard, but the compressed air ones don't pop as easily and will last for weeks. After several weekends of trying, I had a pretty damn good heart.

๛

My ex-husband dropped by one weekend, saw my great work and said, "No one will ever pay you for this. You are wasting your time." No wonder he was an ex. Well, dammit, now I was going to succeed with my balloon work—game on!

I talked to one of the party rental companies in our town that I use frequently, and they thought the balloon business would be good for them and for me as well. They found a balloon sculpture professional in the Bay Area that they hired to come up and give us one day training in making different shapes of sculptures. The rental company was very kind and paid for my share of the training, five hundred bucks, since I had come to them with the idea. The training was very helpful, and the trainer taught us how to make the hearts, grape clusters, trees, and helium arches. I then invested in my own air compressor and made arrangements with a local company to rent a helium tank when needed.

Now, how to actually sell a balloon something? I had a wedding coming up at the local Marriott Hotel and offered my bride two free balloon hearts in her wedding colors, no charge—just for practice and exposure. She agreed and I made two large, ten-foot, pink hearts for either corner of the room. They turned out beautifully, and her mother insisted on paying for them since there had been so many compliments. *Thank you!* Now I had to figure out how much do I charge for these creations? I finally decided by the foot. *So there, you doubters!* I did some advertising in the newspaper and put an ad in the yellow pages under balloons. I was ready for business number three.

This part of the business took off quickly. I started doing balloons for class reunions, parties, baptisms, and restaurants. The most popular was the helium arches. They can be small, doorway size, or huge. I made one that went from one end of a large hall to another. I used fishing line, sixty-pound test or more, for the arch. I blew up the balloons, attaching four, and tied them onto the fishing line. You can make a rainbow of colors by shifting the position of the balloons as you tie on. I held down the ends by tying the fishing line to a brick on each end. I would wrap the bricks in a color to match the balloons. There can be problem if the arch is too big; it will literally lift the bricks off the ground. I was doing a huge arch at the fairgrounds in another town for some kind of a special event they were holding. I would no sooner get one brick down, and the other end would lift. My younger daughter was helping, and her end kept lifting. We just couldn't get the stupid thing grounded. It was arching beautifully and was gorgeous, but if it won't stay down, what the hell? When it was floating about three feet off the ground with my daughter holding one end, I went outside and found a few more bricks. I tied these bricks to the other bricks on each end and finally the damn thing stayed down.

For several years we did balloon releases for New Year's Eve parties at hotels or wineries. I had never done a release before, but how hard can it be? I found a kit for this from the company that I bought the balloons, so I ordered several of the kits. I tried one at home and it worked, so I figured, okay here we go. Basically it's a large net with a slit in the middle. It has a drawstring through the middle of the net that you pull and down the balloons go. The balloons are compressed air so they will fall. We did three set ups for drops one New Year's Eve. I started in the afternoon with the help of my daughters, set up one, explained to the person pulling the cord, did the next, and then the next. A piece of cake! Interesting concept: instead of balloons going up, these were going down.

We did balloon bouquets for restaurants and private parties. Sometimes my car was so full of balloons I couldn't see out the back window. They would float around my car and later my van, and block my vision. As a result, I drove even slower. I finally started stuffing them in large garbage bags until I got to my destination. I was actually pulled over one time by the highway patrol. I thought it was due to the fact I was driving too slow, or had the officer seen my bags and thought I was transporting bodies? I saw the lights behind me, and pulled over. The officer approached my window and I tried to look innocent when I asked what I had done wrong. I knew I wasn't speeding.

He said, "No you weren't speeding, but why did you stop?" He had turned on his light to get around me, and I had just pulled over. "Are you okay? Do you feel sick or need to pull over for any reason?"

"No, sir," I answered, "I'm fine, I just wanted to be polite and follow the rules of the road." He just shook his head and drove off. Did he not appreciate my rule following and good manners? I delivered my balloons and kept the same restaurant account for years.

One of my largest balloon adventures was a huge party at a country club for their banquet room. They wanted large grape clusters ten feet high, eight of them to hang from their ceiling. The ceiling was so high that I didn't have a ladder tall enough, so I had to rent one from a rental company. I made the grape clusters at home over a two-week period. The living room and family room were covered in balloons. I hired one of my young band friends to hang them since I'm afraid of heights. All was going well until I locked my keys inside the van with the grape clusters stacked in the back. We only had three hours to hang these clusters. My young friend was trying to get into the van with a clothes hanger and I was panicking. My youngest daughter had a set of keys but was still in school. We decided the best thing is just to break the van window. But just in time, the hanger worked—we got in and the grapes got hung. I don't know how many close calls I've had in all these years, but too many to count. I think I must be one of those people that love living on the edge, or possibly I just lack common sense.

ᕮᖇᕮ

The next big balloon job, another grape job, was for the City of Napa. Every year the city has a parade for local businesses. Actually, this town has more reasons to close down streets and serve wine than most cities I know. But that's another story. The city wanted twelve grape clusters, four feet each, to hang on the lampposts down First Street. So again I made them two weeks in advance laid them on the living room floor. My kind neighbor helped me hang them at six in the morning so that we would be done by ten, before the event started.

The grapes turned out great; I was becoming a grape expert. What a ring, great on grapes. Why did I get so much balloon business, you ask? I don't think anyone else wanted to do all that work. My girls complained that their fingers were going to drop off form tying. My youngest daughter got so good at it and fast that several times our local florist hired her on Valentine's Day to help with their flower and balloon bouquets. She would come home and soak her fingers in ice water.

Some of these balloon ventures could have been disastrous. We were hired to do two balloon trees for a real estate show at a large hall. The trees are fairly easy to make. I took two plastic pots, spray painted them the color chosen for the theme, gold, black, etc. I then filled the pots with plaster or cement and, as it hardened, I stuck in a dowel for the stem. I had the dowels cut at Home Depot. All I had to do is form the top of the tree with air-compressed balloons in the choice of color. We could even weave real leaves if we chose. Next challenge was to deliver them to the hall and then pick them up at the end of the night. The client had no use for them later. I borrowed a truck from my son in law, laid the trees in the back, covered them with a sheet, and tied a rope over the sheet so they wouldn't blow out. Then, I drove very slowly to the hall. My youngest daughter and her boyfriend came along to help.

All went well, the client was happy, and at ten o'clock that evening, I drove back with the kids to pick them up. We again covered them and tied them down. But apparently I didn't drive slow enough this time, because halfway home on the freeway, the trees flew out the back of the truck onto the road. "Oh my God, we're going to cause a wreck and someone will die." I pulled off the road and looked back to see balloons flying everywhere and the pots bouncing along the road. Well, the kids and I started chasing the flying objects. We were finally able to contain the mangled trees with no wrecks or further damage, just a lot of swerving. Thank goodness this was after the event and not before.

One weekend, I almost missed or messed up a Bar Mitzvah party at a local winery. The parents had hired me to do ten balloon bouquets for the dining tables for this very special day. This was not a big job, and I just had one daughter as my helper. I ordered the eleven-inch balloons in the color chosen and was ready to go. The party was scheduled for a Sunday morning in a small side room at a local winery.

Friday night, I got a phone call from the boy's father confirming we were all set for the next day, Saturday. He just wanted to confirm that I had heard the voice mail that his wife had left earlier on my machine that the party had been moved to Saturday, the next day, since the winery had a date conflict and they had moved the party to a day earlier. He wanted to make sure I was all set.

"Of course, no problem. I'm ready to go." What? No, I am not ready; I don't have my helium tank. I normally pick the tank up the day of the event so that I'm only charged for the tank rental one day and not two.

Ok now what to do? I had the phone number of one of the employees of the rental company and begged him to meet me at ten o'clock that night and give me my tank. "Fine," he said, "but you owe me a dinner." Okay, that's the least I could do. So we met and I got my tank. I had purchased a nozzle a year or so before.

Saturday morning, we arrived, blew up the balloons, and tied them to the centerpieces that the boy's mother had provided for us. I put an extra bouquet on the cake table for good measure and left the winery. Another job well done. What would have happened had the dad not called to remind me of the change in days? I shudder to think about it; the boy's disappointment would've been terrible and my reputation would've been destroyed.

Helpful hint: helium tanks or propane tanks can explode in a vehicle. I did not know this until one day I was delivering some balloons and a PG&E truck and I happened to be backing up at the same time. We backed into each other. No injuries and no blow ups. His truck was heavy so no damage, and my van was old and somewhat beat up, so the little dent didn't matter. My van's name was Chitty Chitty Bang Bang, by the way, a member of the family; she lived and worked for twenty-one years. Thank goodness there was no serious damage. The PG&E driver did notice the tanks in the back of my van and told me that I should not be traveling around with them since they can explode after an impact or accident. Great, now I learn these wonderful facts after hauling these damned things for years.

I did continue with the balloon business for several years after that. I still have the air compressor in my garage. You never know if I may feel the urge again.

Chapter 6:

The Bridal Store

IN 1996, I GOT REMARRIED AND IN THE NEXT BREATH opened a bridal gown store. It went down like this.

I met my next husband after being single for eight years. I honestly didn't have time to date, as you can see from the previous chapters. Between the weddings, accounting, taxes, catering, balloons, and daughters and their activities, I barely had time to floss. Besides, who needs to be married when I get to be a part of all these wonderful weddings?

I started doing line dancing with the neighbor who had lost his wife. He said he just couldn't stand to be home alone, so he started hanging out at my house after work. He had never done any dancing and said he really didn't know how. A local bar in town started giving line dancing lessons once or twice a week. It was country music most nights. So we signed up. My youngest had just started college, so I had time on my hands. My friend, I will call Ted, and I started dancing a couple of times a week. Soon other friends joined us, and we danced locally and in towns close by. In no time, we were dancing three to four nights a week. Ted would help me if I had weddings on the weekend, by again cutting, slicing, and loading, or help me hang or drop off balloons.

One Saturday night, Ted and I and eight other friends were dancing at a country western bar in a town about thirty minutes away. Dancing had become our new love, and it's great exercise. Anyway, we saw this man sitting alone at a table not far from ours. He would smile, and I would smile back. Finally as I walked by his table, I asked him why he wasn't dancing. He responded he didn't know how but had just stopped by for a beer. We asked him to join our table. During the table conversation, Jim happened to mention to Ted that he had lost his wife to cancer the previous year; both had that loss in common.

We continued to chat, and he invited me to dance when a slow dance came up. At the end of the night, he asked for my phone number and I gave it to him. Later, I asked why me? There were lots of single, middle-aged women hanging out. He responded, "I love a woman in tight jeans."

A week later, Jim called me. I had planned to go dancing that night, and I gave him the name of our local pub. Jim dropped by and we got better acquainted. We had dinner the next week and started to see each other on a regular basis. A year later we were married. I continued doing my weddings, catering, and working during the year. I also did some income taxes during March and April since I felt an obligation to my long time tax clients. Honesty, I really didn't have time for dating, so it was either get married or break up. Jim owned a home in Fairfield and I owned mine in Napa, so we sold both homes and bought a new one together in Napa. I was not going to leave Napa, period. Jim was still going to commute to his job in finance management in the Bay Area.

While we were dating, I did some catering jobs, and Jim offered to come and help. I'll tell you right now, he can't cook and still doesn't, but he can peel, chop, and clean up. He's a great dishwasher. The first job he came to help out was a summer wedding on a very hot day. One of the items on the buffet was a tomato basil salad tray. I had brought several large crates of tomatoes. The tomatoes were a hit, and the tray of sliced tomatoes kept disappearing. I asked Jim to go to the store down the street for more tomatoes. He bought a flat and brought them back. He no sooner got in the door and I sent him back for more. He cleaned the store out of tomatoes, and the owner asked him what he thought he was doing with all those tomatoes. I honestly think some of the guests were swiping

tomatoes to take home for later. Did the guests have baggies in their pockets or purses? Who knows?

By the time Jim got finished doing the dishes and mopping the floor, I thought for sure he'd dump me. But by God, he chose to stick around.

We were married in August. One week after we were married a lady that owned the local bridal store called me and told me she was selling the store and retiring. She asked if I was interested in buying it. I had done the bridal shows with her in previous years. I discussed this with Jim, and he told me if it's something that I wanted to do and thought I could do, then he was all in. He liked to relax and play golf on the weekends, but he would love to help if he could. My weekends were more work than play. Was he in for a treat and a new living experience? I was introduced to the game of golf on our honeymoon, and I still love to play to this day. Although just like on our honeymoon, I do not take golf advice from him or anyone! I do it my way, or not at all. Could that be one of my problems—not taking advice?

I gave notice at the accounting job that I had held for years. I also told Jim I would give up the catering but not the balloon business, and do fewer weddings a year. I would do taxes only for family. The store would be open seven days a week since we were located in a town center and our lease required us to be open every day. We did an inventory of the bridal store and took possession in less than two weeks. The store had some inventory but was seriously depleted since the old owner had not wanted to spend the money to purchase new gowns and inventory.

We now needed new stock, wedding gowns, bridesmaids, veils, lingerie, etc. The week before we took ownership, Jim and I went to Las Vegas to a bridal show to purchase what we needed. Twice a year shows are held in Las Vegas, Chicago, New York, Dallas, and other large cities to sell their products for fall and spring. The two shows are normally held in October for the spring line, and March for the fall line. So here we are at the end of September, and we needed to go to the show closest to us, which happened to be in Las Vegas. I have to say it was exciting. I had never been to Las Vegas. Talk about a place to party, if you have time. I did squeeze in an hour or two at the quarter poker machines. You have to give yourself a break once in a while.

We spent four days buying wedding gowns, bridesmaid dresses, mother of the bride, shoes, veils, lingerie, everything. What we didn't know is that each line, company, or brand has a minimum number of gowns that you need to purchase to carry their line. Most require eight to ten gowns from each line. There are lots and lots of great designers out there. I could find maybe two or three I liked in each line, but not the whole line. I also wanted to carry at least five lines in various price ranges. We finally made our choices between these lines. Jim and I don't happen to agree on styles, and this caused several fights during the week. After several years of our disagreements at these shows, one of the sales representatives told us that they had decided that if Darlene likes the dress and Jim hates it, it will be a top seller. I was going to say, "What do men know about fashion?" but look at the great designers that are men.

It is exhausting work, spending money. The first night, we could hardly move, and when I asked Jim if we could go out for dinner, he said, "You can't afford to eat, you spent twenty-five thousand bucks today." But he did feed me. It's hard to spend that kind of money and not know if your inventory will sell or not. You also have to buy the sample gowns twice a year as the styles change, if you want to keep the line. If a gown discontinues, it needs to sell it off the rack. That's not easy either. I began to think we were getting in over our heads. Yes, Jim and I both had experience in business, but no experience in retail. But dammit, I was not going to admit I was worried, never.

The store walls were being painted while we were gone, pale pink, and the carpets cleaned. When we returned, we were ready to go with the stock we had, and the new shipment would come in a month or two. We soon got into a system. I would work in the store ten to six and Jim would come after work to steam gowns and dye shoes. In those days, the satin shoes were dyed to match the bride's dress and often the bridesmaid's dresses. We bought the dye kits from a company called Colorific. The process is simple: the dye is already mixed in bottles, and you can mix together two or more colors to make the colors you want. Just like mixing paint –easy. Well, not always. The colors may look right inside, but off or terrible outside. Especially, ivory or beige, which can turn pink outside. We ruined many pairs of shoes trying to get the right color.

On weekends Jim would come in and vacuum, clean the bathroom, and help me with window displays. Dummies are fairly light but awkward to handle. Arms and hands were always falling off. Jim would steam the new gowns as they arrived, and we would pick a new gown to display in the window. One Saturday Jim was in the window moving a naked mannequin when this woman stormed into our store yelling at us to cover the disgusting nude woman in the window. When we laughed, thinking she was kidding, she totally went off on us, calling us sick perverts. We later changed to black cloth mannequins—no head or legs, just bodies. The mannequins we had inherited were actually scary looking with wild eyes.

Our only time off was to go to Vegas for the biannual shows and sometimes Los Angeles for other markets, lingerie, and formalwear. Prom and formalwear became a big part of our business. We have three high schools in our town, and we adopted the policy of one prom dress per school. When we sold a prom dress we made note of the style, designer, and color, the girl's name, and her school. Then we would order the dress or sale off the rack. If another girl from that school wanted the same dress, we declined to sell it to her, telling her someone else already had the same dress. The girls knew they would be the only one with that dress for their special night. We normally sold about two hundred dresses during prom season. We also donated dresses to the schools for the girls that could not afford to purchase a dress. These prom dresses can sell from one hundred and fifty to four hundred dollars. We also donated wedding gowns to the local Community Projects store.

One Saturday Jim was working in the store when two mothers asked why a man was in the store. I simply told them that Jim was gay so not to worry. He still laughs about it, but after that, no one cared. The company that Jim had been working for in the Bay Area asked him to locate out of state for a move up with the company, but he chose to take an early retirement since we had a lease and we just couldn't move. There was no way in hell I was leaving Napa.

In the first year of the store it was all hands on deck with my daughters helping in when they could. Our youngest daughter would try to make it home a few weekends a month to pitch in. I was speaking to Rhonda the other night, and she reminded me of some of the more unpleasant encounters.

One weekend when she was working a lady was trying to return a velvet dress that she had purchased from the previous owner. The woman had bought the dress at least the year before, and she thought as new owners we might be fooled or stupid enough to fall for her story; naïve yes, stupid maybe. The woman had tried to iron the velvet dress, which most people know that you can't iron velvet. If you try it, then turn it inside out. The iron had crushed down the velvet and left a bald spot. She insisted to my older daughter Debbie that she receive her money back since the dress was ruined. Debbie explained that the dress came from the prior owner and we were not responsible. The woman continued to argue and draw the attention of other shoppers. Debbie went to get her younger sister Rhonda from the back room. "You deal with her, she's nasty." Debbie is the peacemaker/prankster in the family. Her two younger sisters are tougher or have a bigger set of…well, you know what.

Rhonda also tried to reason with the woman that we had not sold the dress and were not responsible for the damage to it. It was obvious that the situation was not going to be resolved that day. So Rhonda and the lady decided to leave the dress for me to see when I got back from my Vegas buying trip.

The following week, we settled this dispute by giving this woman a fifty-dollar gift certificate for a new purchase in the store, but no refund. We were about to find out that the prior owner had given out and sold many gift certificates. So we, the gullible new owners, were expected to respect all of these certificates and credits. In our purchasing contract, we had made it clear that we were not responsible for the previous debts or obligations, and we had not purchased her receivables or payables. However, the customers did not give a hoot if we were responsible or not and continued to push us to accept these gift certificates. We did end up honoring many of them just to be nice and encourage new business. It was becoming more obvious that we had a lot to learn about retail and customer service.

Most of our customers were pleasant and frequent shoppers; if not for weddings gowns, then for lingerie, formalwear, and prom. One wedding gown per customer seems to be the norm. However, we did sell three gowns to one bride. She planned to change gowns throughout the night, and wow, that worked for us.

We also had repeat prom girls year after year. We did have one unfortunate prom experience. We sold a dress to a young senior three weeks before her prom. We pressed and bagged the dress, and the young girl took the dress with her. Two days before the prom the young girl and her mother came into the store asking to return the dress for a full cash refund. The dress smelt of perfume and I asked if possibly the dress had been worn to one of the other school proms or had it been worn at all? Why was she returning the dress? It had looked absolutely perfect on her. Her mother proceeded to tell me that the date, the girl's boyfriend, had dumped her daughter and she would no longer be going to the prom.

I tried to be sympathetic in my response, "I'm sorry, they broke up but the dress appears to have been worn." The mother proceeded to scream at me that her daughter's life was ruined and she was humiliated that she was not going to the prom, and I was making it worse. Yeah, yeah. The mother then started crying and the daughter started yelling that I had made her mother cry. Oh my gosh, besides being a terrible person, I had ruined this young woman's love life;

I'm going to hell for sure. The mother then threatened me that her husband was an attorney and would sue me. This situation was quickly getting out of control. Finally, I told her that I would give her a store credit. I asked her to please calm down as other customers were watching this big scene. Then, to my surprise,, the red-faced, irate mother picked up the dress and threw it in my face. Great, another crazy customer. I had not realized this was such a physical business.

We had very few wedding gowns returned. Most of our bride's would pick out their style and color from our samples in the store, and then we would order the dress in their size and color option. It would not be easy to sell their dress to another customer, if the wedding cancelled. Our contract explained this, and it was never really an issue. If for some reason the wedding did not go through, the bride could keep the dress or try to sell it online. If this groom didn't work out, maybe the next one would.

☉\☉

One of our very sweet brides was having her final fitting with one of our three seamstresses when she started crying and said, "I'm not sure I can go through with this."

I asked the bride if there was a problem while I handed over a box of tissues. "Yes," she said, "I found out that Tom (her husband-to-be) had a one night stand with my maid of honor. They both swear it's over and it meant nothing, but I'm not sure I believe them." She wasn't sure that she could go through with it. Her mother was with her and had told her repeatedly that they were glad to cancel the wedding, take the loss in money, and do whatever it took to make their daughter happy.

I totally agreed with Mom. "If he's not faithful now, what makes you think he'll be faithful after you're married? What about the friend, the back stabbing bitch?" Of course, I do try to give sound advice, but perhaps I should mind my own business. I did get a call from the bride's mom a few days later, and yes, the wedding was off but someday that beautiful dress would be worn. In my opinion, it was a very smart decision. A year later, the dress was worn by our bride with a new, nicer, and faithful groom.

We found that Kleenex, champagne, and hugs were a necessity in the store. Our brides also had visitation rights with their dresses. Most brides preferred to keep their gowns in the back room of our store, protectively wrapped in a white dress bag. During wedding season, we had up to one hundred and fifty gowns hanging. These were kept alphabetically under the bride's name and wedding date. Our brides would pop in from time to time to try on the dress, make sure it still fit, or just bring a friend in to see the dress. We were always happy to have these visits and bring in new future brides.

We kept the store going for eleven years, moving to a larger location for a three-year lease. We wanted to be able to do tuxedo rentals and invitations that we couldn't do in the other location due to a clause in our lease. Two stores in our old mall had tuxedos and invitations, so were limited in what we could sell. Of course when we moved, we had to paint again, build dressing rooms, tile floors, and clean carpets. We also had to keep the other store going while we moved into the new store. We would transport the wedding gowns at night in my van, Chitty.

The move went well, and we enjoyed the larger space. The tuxedo rental business was very good and our employees got very good at measuring the men as well as the women. Our oldest daughter Debbie came to work for us part time in the mornings. She would call in orders, check on existing orders, and track gown shipments.

We all learned a great deal about the business, such as how to measure a bride and pick the style best suited to the bride and her party. Bridal gowns run small, so a bride might be a size eight but might need a ten or maybe a twelve in her wedding gown. Unfortunately the bride may not want to hear this. They will tell you they will lose the weight, and please order their normal size. Helpful hint: be realistic. You may lose some weight, but not likely enough, and why make yourself miserable trying? The dress is easier to take in than out. The better the designers and the more expensive dresses, the smaller the seams and the harder to let out. We had so many brides in tears because they didn't lose the weight, and our seamstresses did their best to let out seams. We had several great seamstresses working full time during bridal season. One sweet bride told me to order the size I thought she needed, but to cut out the tag with the size when the dress arrived in the store. I put my hand over the contract when she signed it so she couldn't see the size. She said, "If I can't see the size, then I won't be depressed." She had a good point, and I cut out the label when her dress arrived.

Another helpful hint for brides shopping for the perfect gown: bring your mother or one other person. Do not bring the whole party. Fights often break out. Jealousy can rear its head, nasty comments can fly, and the bride will be in tears. We served champagne to our brides while shopping, anything to calm the nerves.

We have literally had fistfights in the store. One bride's sister, her maid of honor, threw hot coffee on the bride and told her the dress she had picked for her bridesmaids was ugly. She accused the bride of picking the dress to make her look fat and that she had never loved her. Debbie had to ask them to step outside since we had white wedding gowns hanging on racks nearby. Bridesmaids can be very nasty when provoked. I never saw this with groomsmen; they were glad to wear anything the groom picked out.

One mother chose her daughter's wedding gown and gave the ride absolutely no say in the matter. This young woman had tried on four to five gowns that looked great on her. The bride, who was on the larger side, wanted to compliment her assets and I agreed. She looked good in the halter styles or off the shoulder, and she had a lovely neck that we wanted to emphasize. The bride found one that she truly loved, and Mom said, "Absolutely not, you look like a tramp." The bride was in tears, and Mom was in my face when I told her how beautiful her daughter looked. She told me that since she was paying the bride would wear what she told her to wear. Mom then proceeded to go through the racks and pulled out a dress that was very conservative, to say the least. It was a dress that I had inherited when I bought the store, high neck, long sleeves—yuck. I should have donated it. Mom told me that she'd have it altered to fit her daughter, and that was that. The bride left in tears, still begging her mother. My heart went out to the poor girl. There are so many flattering styles for all sized brides. Why shouldn't they all feel beautiful?

We also had our issues with thefts, especially in the downtown mall store. We had starting carrying some high end cocktail dresses and formal wear for some of our loyal customers. There are several black tie events in the Valley, wine auctions, film festivals, etc. We had requests for formal-wear as well as the prom and wedding gowns. Jim and I started to go to clothing markets in Los Angeles that carried some of the nicer lines of cocktail and formal wear. We found four or five lines that were beautiful and within our price range. If we paid four hundred dollars for a nice dress, it would retail for eight hundred to eight hundred and fifty.

We would order in two or three of each dress in various sizes. Some of our customers would come to the store in advance of the event and asked to find a gown in their size for a big event. So when we went to market, we had this client in mind when we looked at the various designers. I would also order dresses for me while at market, one for the store, one for me, etc. "Why not?" I told Jim. "After all, it's wholesale." Now I just have to find the time and a place to wear it.

Soon we had some serious money invested in these dresses, but they were selling and we had happy customers. I had just gotten in a shipment of beautiful new black dresses from a new and pricey designer. I was so excited and hung them in a place of prominence by the front window. I was going to call my favorite customers to come in and take a look at the new shipment.

On Saturday morning I got to the store at ten just as one of our employees arrived. I was excited to show her the new stock. Within fifteen minutes we were busy with ladies looking through the racks. There was some kind of a street fair happening on the street out front of our store, so we were getting people just window shopping. I walked over the rack where I had hung four new black dresses, when I noticed that there were three empty hangers with one dress on the three hangers. What the heck? Where were the new dresses? I started to panic and rushed to other racks to find more dresses missing. I said to our employee, "Did you move any dresses or hangers?" No, she had not. There were three women still in the store, just browsing. We had asked them if they needed help, but no, just looking. All I could think was that the thief had to still be in the store. So I said to our employee in a very loud voice, "By the way, Jim installed secret cameras last night since we've had some merchandise missing."

Immediately, two of these women left the store. I told our employee to call Jim at home and tell him to get down here, now! The third lady continued to walk around, but I noticed her bending over especially close to the fuller rack of wedding gowns. Then the woman left, her arms were empty except for a small purse. I decided to follow her, but I quickly lost her in the street crowd.

I went back to the store and went through rack by rack. At least eight dresses were missing, and approximately three thousand dollars worth of inventory gone. I was sick to my stomach; we can't afford that kind of loss. Jim arrived and we called the police.

When the officer arrived, he confirmed what we had thought; that there wasn't much they or we could do. He told us that there was a ring of women that were thought to be involved in clothing and jewelry thefts around town. They would put the stolen goods under their clothes to get them out of the store and then would sell them once a month at a flea market. We might want to check out the flea market and install either a real camera or a fake one and a mirror. I hated to do that. It looks like you don't trust your customers, but after that, we had no choice.

Sunday morning, I got to the store early to vacuum and straighten the dressing rooms. When I moved a rack of wedding gowns, I saw something black sticking out under the rack, and when I moved the rack I found two of our black missing dresses. Apparently the third woman had these two dresses under her dress and when I told our employee about the new camera, the lady had bent down and shoved the dresses under the rack and quickly left the store. I had noticed in the last few months empty hangers or two dresses on one hanger, but I never thought that they were stolen, but maybe just moved by an employee. How naïve I was in hindsight.

Jim ordered a fake camera with a blinking red light and a big round mirror to hang from the ceiling. Once these were installed, we had no more thefts in the downtown store. Jim and I did go to the local flea market but never saw any of our dresses. What is the old adage? "You win some, you lose some." However, we didn't win any, but lost some. Double dammit.

When we moved to the new store on the north side of town we installed the same mirror and camera. As far as I know, in that store we only had one theft and that also happened on a weekend. We carried a very nice line of lingerie, bras, panties, etc. We kept the lingerie in a separate section of the store, away from the gowns and in an area with smaller dressing rooms to allow for privacy. On this Saturday morning, a young woman came into the store and started looking at the lingerie. She was mumbling to herself and she wandered from rack to rack. She pulled out several bras and panties sets in red and black. I offered to put them aside for her so she could continue to look. She declined. Jim was hanging gowns in the back and the other employees were not scheduled in yet. Then all of a sudden, this young woman ran out of the store carrying the lingerie with her.

"Jim! Jim, run after her!" I yelled. Jim came out while I was standing out front watching which way she ran. I told him the quick story and said, "Jim, follow her. I'll call the police." Jim followed her for maybe six blocks—she ran, and he ran.

The officer came to the store and I explained the situation and told him that my husband was following her. "Ma'am," he said, "that's not a good idea. She could be dangerous."

"Officer, this is expensive lingerie, and he better be able to handle himself," I responded back. The officer then headed off in the direction that both the woman and Jim had gone. The officer did find them, and he brought Jim and the woman back to the store and the lingerie to be identified. Yes, it was our lingerie, but it was filthy after our thief had dropped it several times during the chase, so I decided to toss it. The woman had several priors and encounters with the police, but she also was not the most stable woman, and we chose not to file charges. Her family would keep an eye on her and she was receiving professional help, so why make it worse? Just keep her out of my lingerie, and I'm good with letting her go.

We had a variety of customers including prom and formalwear shoppers but most were brides looking for that perfect gown. Our busiest season was right after Christmas when brides got their engagement rings. The day after Thanksgiving and the week after Christmas were crazy busy days in the store. All hands on deck. We could be there from nine in the morning until nine at night. The holidays were a fun time at the store, putting up lights in the windows and Christmas trees inside. Candy and champagne were handed out to customers during these festive times.

I remember one year we volunteered to do a float in the Christmas parade. We borrowed a pickup from a friend and covered it in battery operated twinkle lights. We put a small, lighted tree in the back with a bride in a full gown sitting on a small stool. We had the name of our store on both doors of the truck. If I say so myself, it looked pretty snazzy. We also had a flower girl and a ring bearer walking behind the truck carrying baskets of wrapped Christmas candy and throwing to the crowd.

The day and the parade seemed to be a hit until the rains came. The parade had three blocks to go when the downpour hit. Our bride and the kids kept up a brave front. Our bride continued to smile and wave, looking more and more liked a drowned white rat. By the time the truck and our parade goers got back to the store, they were a mess. The wedding gown was ruined, the bride soaked and the kids happy. Small children, for some reason, love being in the rain. The bride was a very good sport and a friend of Debbie's, and the little ones were my grandchildren, bribed with candy. The good news from this rained out disaster was that a picture of our damp bride made the front page of our newspaper. Great advertising, and it didn't cost a cent.

Other brides would shop before they became engaged. The same Brides would come in week after week to try on their dress that she would order as soon as he proposed. One bride that I became very fond of came in every week with the same question: why hadn't he proposed yet? He was one smart guy who I did get to know when we finally fitted him for his tux. He took our bride on a trip to Hawaii and she called," Be ready to order the dress, he's going to propose." Nope, she came back with no ring. Then a few months later, he took her for a weekend away. She called again, "This is it, order the dress." No again. By this time she's crying and ready to give up. Then one night he said the sink had a leak and would she climb under the sink with him to help and hand him a wrench. You guessed it, he proposed under the sink with the ring in this dirty hand. She was back in the store the next day, and we ordered the dress.

We developed some great friendships through the store. We sold the girls their prom dress and then their wedding gown. I still see some of our brides in the grocery store or around town. I miss that part of it. I also learned about the best styles for body types and gown colors. I was thrilled when gowns started coming in colors—oyster, champagne, ivory, and even multi-colored. I carried more gowns of color than white. White can wash out even the most beautiful bride. I brought in a red wedding gown for one season just to have in my window for the holidays. It sold the next day. I asked my customer to please let me keep it until after Christmas, but she was adamant and she took it that day. We also learned that gowns that sell in California and New York and the East Coast won't sell in the Midwest. The styles are very different; strapless is a great seller here, but not in the Midwest states. I could not sell a long sleeved, fluffy dress here, but they couldn't sell the sleeker look there.

We also made friends with store owners all over the country, and we were able to travel to Spain and England on a buying trip and exchange ideas and design thoughts. We could also help each other locate gowns or lines that we did not carry in our store.

We finally closed the store after eleven years. Our rent was going up and more space was being added to the complex, so we decided it was time to close. I could go back to coordinating full time. Internet buying was also hurting business. Brides could try on gowns in our store, but then order direct online. We saw the writing on the wall and knew it was time to say goodbye to that part of our life.

Chapter 7:

Balloon Business Comes to a Close

I HAD KEPT THE BALLOON BUSINESS GOING FOR A YEAR or so after we took over the bridal store. We had less time, but I wanted to take care of the local clients that I had. It had been a real upper for years.

Jim was willing to help me with this and soon learned how to blow up balloons, tie, and assemble the hearts, trees, and arches. The restaurants were still easy to handle with delivery of bouquets for special occasions, holidays—Valentine's Day was a biggie. The more time consuming jobs were the balloon drops and arches for weddings, graduation proms, etc. Finally, there were two events that pushed Jim over the edge, and down went the balloon business.

New Year's Eve was always big for balloons, and we had three jobs on one New Year's Eve. We left the store with our great employees at two o'-clock in the afternoon and headed to our first job. This was at a resort in the valley that I had done for years. They wanted balloons to the ceiling. This is a helium balloon in two or three sizes with strings that flowed to the ceiling and stayed all night over the dance floor. I had ordered the bal-loons for all the jobs and had two large tanks in the van. We took one helper and arrived on the property, and we started blowing and tying. We added a spray into each balloon that helps it stay up longer. We finished in two hours or so. It looked great and we left for the next job.

My next job was balloon bouquets for a restaurant that I had been doing for years. No problem—blow them up, tie them, scatter the bouquets around the room, and we're done.

Job number three was the killer. This job was also balloons to the ceiling just like job number one. It was at a private estate, and they wanted the balloons with no strings in the client's choice of color. What we didn't know was that the owner wanted a solid ceiling of balloons with no part of the ceiling showing. What she didn't tell us was that the ceiling was peaked, curved, and higher in the middle. So the balloons would all gather in the center, and it was taking three times the amount of balloons I had thought and three times the size. Every time the lady came into the room, she would say, "More, more, I need more balloons." We finally covered that damn ceiling, but I used every balloon and all the helium I had in the van. So much for profit on that job. She paid, and we left. Just a note: she called me the next year to do her balloons again. I said, "No thank you. I'm out of business."

We had plans to join friends for a late dinner and we headed home to change. We could make it if we hurried. As we were leaving the house, the phone rang. We got a call from the resort where we had done the balloons to the ceiling, the first job. The manager said the balloons are coming down. "Oh, my gosh, we tied them well. They should stay up for ten to twelve hours!" I said frantically. So Jim said he would head back up and I would meet him at the restaurant. Well an hour later, Jim arrived at dinner.

"So…what happened? How could they have fallen?" I asked.

Jim just shrugged and said, "Three balloons fell. Out of four hundred, just three fell. I replaced the three and left." The manager had panicked. They also called the next year, and I again said no.

We were asked to do balloon Christmas trees for a local stage production. The trees would be twelve feet high. The client ordered two trees, one for each side of the stage. I gave him a price for what I thought it would cost based on the footage. He did try to barter the price down, but we were firm—that's a lot of balloons. We used the pots again, filled with plaster sprayed gold, added a dowel in each, and started building: green balloons, five inches, tied in clusters, smaller at the top and getting larger at the bottom. I added some small red and gold balloons in places to be ornaments. We built them in our home, which had tall ceilings, and it took me about six days after the store closed at night. They were beautiful. I had never attempted something so difficult, and we were proud parents. We delivered the first one to the theatre at the time requested. We had to deliver one at a time since they were so big. We could only fit one in the van. Even then, the tree hung out the back of the van, and I ended up riding in the back of the van holding onto the tree so it wouldn't fall out. I had been down that road before.

We carried the tree in and set it up on the stage. I told the client we were heading back for the other tree. He said," Gee, I didn't realize it would be so big, so I'm just going to take the one and pay for one."

Well, so much for that. I should have gotten a contract. We had done all that work for half the money, and we still had one very big tree at home. The other tree went to the store for additional décor. Another lesson learned.

I think the balloon job that finally finished Jim off was the high school graduation. I had done balloon work on a smaller scale for two of our high schools, dances, proms, etc. but never anything as large as this. They wanted two balloon arches, fifty feet high each, for each end of the football field at the goal posts for the graduates to walk under and onto the field. These were to be done in the school colors. Since these were going to be outside and not blow over or be knocked down, we chose to use white PVC pipe, which is sturdier. I ordered the pipe and the balloons. Again, because these were so big and long, we built them at home with compressed air. They would stand and arch because of the heavier and sturdier pipe. I normally would use helium for the arch. Jim and I took the first one to the school, no problem. We used tent stakes to anchor each end of the first arch. I dropped Jim off and took off home for the second arch. When I got back, the wind had picked up and was whipping the arch back and forth. It was almost touching the ground before it went the other way. There was no way to make this large arch anchor.

We still had to put up the other arch and the grads were getting ready to line up. The bleachers were filling up. We did the best we could, but all I could see was Jim fighting these monsters in the wind, and all I could do was laugh. They were pretty and big enough, but they just kept blowing this way and that. I was worried one of the poor grads would get knocked over by our flying monster. We apologized to the man in charge, and quickly left. We both felt bad, but what can you do? I don't know if a sturdier pipe would have worked. If kids hadn't been walking under it, the waving motion wouldn't have been so bad. The school also called again the next year, and again, I said no.

After a very quick discussion, we decided to retire the balloon business. The calls continued to come in for the next year. So sad…it was fun while it lasted. Well, if I ever get bored, I still have my air compressor.

Chapter 8:

Wedding Coordination Continues

WHAT THEY SAY ABOUT WHEN A DOOR CLOSES, a window opens must be true. Within months of closing the store, I got a call from one of the caterers that I always enjoyed working with. They were getting very busy, and the lady that managed their wedding business was getting too busy to oversee the weddings and be in charge of the food too. Would I like to be their onsite coordinator for all the weddings they booked? This was about twenty years ago. I said I would love to. Great timing.

I worked with this caterer for five years or so until the owner sold to one of his chefs. By that time I was too busy to help them as much as I used to. I loved working with their staff and learned so much from them. I saw the other real professional side of catering, with huge events, lots of staff, and very sophisticated menus. I learned what sized linens go on which sized tables. I learned about glassware, and how much to order per guest count. I quickly learned how long each course takes to clear and serve and how to serve. I was blessed to learn from this wonderful woman who has since passed.

By working with them, I also did some amazing weddings for some very renowned clients. One of the most memorable weddings I did with them was at a private estate for a local winery owner. The wedding was to be held outside in the fall on a beautiful spot on a hill in the middle of the vineyards.

The couple and both families were great to work with. The rehearsal went well and the planning was right on target. However, the day before the wedding the weather looked like rain. The bride's family quickly rented an open sided tent for dinner service with two long tables running down the middle. Umbrellas were brought in, and we were ready for the worst.

It started raining the next day as guests were arriving. The guests were to be taken from the entrance to the wedding site by a small shuttle bus. As I was walking back down the hill to chat with the shuttle bus, I noticed that a pickup truck had slid in the mud and was lying on its side and blocking the road. We asked a couple of the winery workers to have it pulled or pushed to the side of the road, but it became apparent that the shuttle would not make it up the hill. We did have a golf cart on site, so we began to shuttle guests up to the ceremony site by golf cart. This took longer, but hey, it worked. We got everyone seated and the ceremony went great. The poor bride and groom were drenched by this time. They didn't want to use the umbrellas and spoil the photos. They were heroes, standing in the rain and smiling.

The cocktail hour was under the tent, and they guests were quickly served with great wine and appetizers. During the cocktail hour, I was trying to fix the place cards that had blown over by the wind and the rain and into the vineyards. I wasn't able to find all the cards but was winging it and was able to finally seat the guests for dinner. Not necessarily in the assigned spot, but good enough; everyone did have a seat. I had been told that one prominent winery owner and his wife would not be staying for dinner, so place cards had not been made for them. But after the ceremony, this gentleman told me that he and his wife had decided to stay for dinner after all. He wanted to know if this would be a problem.

I assured him it was not and took him and his wife to a spot at the table close to the bride's parents. I also told him that their place cards had blown into the vineyards. So, of course I had to adjust guests all the way down the table, pull up two extra chairs, and ask for two more place settings. I didn't want to alienate any guests or worse, family members. This is when the "fake it till you make it" applies.

The guests were gracious and kind through all of this, and dinner was served as promptly as possible with the changes and the wind and rain pelting from all sides of the tent. The staff was soaked since they had to go back and forth between the tent kitchen and the guest's tent. I tried to escape inside the tent kitchen whenever I could if just to wipe the water off my face and push back my matted hair.

Dancing was not as popular as it might have been if it was not raining, but the hardy souls hung in there. The bride and groom kept up the good spirits all evening. When it was time for them to leave, the car that was to be used couldn't get up the hill, so the bride and groom left on the back of a John Deere tractor. What a photo op. The guests went down the hill to their cars in the golf cart. I went home, soaked but happy, and threw away the pantsuit that I had been wearing. The mud would never come out of my pants.

I continued doing weddings with this caterer and without them throughout the valley. We did wineries, at least those allowed in our valley, resorts, hotels, and some private homes. I met some great vendors along the way, caterers, florists, DJ's, musicians, bakers, etc. Some of these vendors I have worked with for over thirty years and continue to work with today. It really is a team effort, and I love the team that I am fortunate enough to work with.

I've had the pleasure of working with some amazing couples, some famous, not so famous, and just nice, kind people. When we have weddings with the more famous, actors, politicians, sports figures, we often sign a non-disclosure agreement. Every guest deserves their privacy during the evening. No autographs or pictures unless authorized. We have had to hire extra staffing or security for some of these couples to take care of special needs that they may have. A few of these kind celebrities have let me have photos and even use them on my website.

I was fortunate enough to do the wedding for two Broadway producers from New York. It was done at a local winery, and it was amazing. The wedding was done as a play with live actors performing on stage. The costumes and actors came from the East Coast or San Francisco. Experts in lighting, photography, and videography were brought in. The flowers, tables, and linens were of the best quality and fabulous colors. It was an enchanting evening. I think I enjoyed it as much as the guests. I should also mention that one of my grooms had also worked for me when he was in high school and a band member. Both he and his brother had worked for me. I was so honored to be a part of his wedding, and so proud of him and his great success.

I have counted over 1,400 weddings that I have done in the past thirty-five years. Each wedding is different and exciting. We have done weddings with horses, falcons, and dogs. We have had lion dancers, ballroom dancers, casino nights, caricature artists, and more themes than you can imagine. We have had snow cone machine, frosé machines, and popcorn machines, and oh yes, smoke machines.

We did one wedding on Halloween that was a mystery theme where the guests had to solve a murder. We had a corpse in the corner covered with a black cloth until time to announce the murder. The corpse was made of straw dressed in casual cloths and blood on his chest. During dinner the DJ announced that everyone should remain in their seats, a murder had occurred. "Please check your table to see if you are missing a knife or if you note something unusual," he said. Where was each guest during the last twenty minutes? The corpse was then uncovered. Every table got a chance to guess the name of the killer until one of the groomsmen confessed. It was fun, a change of pace, and fit perfectly with the night, rainy and cold.

At the end of the night when we were leaving the winery, Jim, myself, and one of the winery staff heard a *whoo whoo* sounds coming from the trees by the lawn. The young woman, the winery manager, asked me, "Do you hear that? It sounds like an owl."

I told her it was probably one of the staff hanging out trying to scare us. After all, it's Halloween. When the sound continued, and seemed to be coming from two different trees, we decided to investigate. Jim shown a flashlight up into first tree and the next large oak tree, and there were two sets of eyes in each tree. Two owls! Unbelievable, and on Halloween too. I had never seen an owl at this property before and have never seen one since that night. The timing was amazing; however, we decided, this was just too freaky and a very weird coincidence. We quickly got the hell out of there.

Another great wedding was a Disney theme. The bride was dressed as Beauty, the groom as the Beast, although I have to say he was too handsome to be a beast. Each of the bridesmaids was a Disney character, right down to their dresses and the color of their hair. One bridesmaid had dyed her hair red to be Ariel. Each bouquet reflected her character. The tables were each a different Disney table: Lady and the Tramp, Mary Poppins, etc. done by a florist whom I dearly love and work with much of the time, and they did an amazing job. Everyone stayed in character the entire night. It was truly magical.

One amazing wedding was fabulous with flowers, draping, and lighting. The groom's mother owned a decorating company that did high end events, horse shows, political events, etc. She brought in her own team to do the décor. It took two days of draping and lighting, and it was brilliant. The flowers alone were over a hundred thousand dollars. I have never seen anything like it since. What made it even nicer was that the mother was great to work with, humble, and willing to give and take advice. My couples see this wedding on my website and want to duplicate it, but when I tell them the price, they quickly decide against it.

I could go on with all the amazing weddings we've been honored to be a part of. I actually saw one of our guests on TV last night on a rerun of *Murder She Wrote*. He was the officiant and a friend of the couple that we did a wedding for a few years ago. He was an actor, so he did a great job as the officiant, and he was fun and a pleasure to work with. He still looks great. I said, "Jim, that's Michael, from the wedding." He invited us out for a drink after the wedding. We didn't go, but at least we were invited.

Some of these celebrities are very kind and will offer autographs or photos with the staff or vendors. We always honor their privacy, but that doesn't stop the staff from gathering in the kitchen to gossip about the celebrity's dress, date, or how fabulous they look, how different from their look in movies or television. We have been fortunate to work with some amazing professional athletes and even if I don't always understand their sport, I am always excited to see them on TV.

Chapter 9:

Cakes, Flowers, and Décor

I THOUGHT I SHOULD THROW THIS IN about décor, cakes, and flowers. There are many ways to add décor or spruce up the ceremony and reception site. Some venues are so beautiful that they don't need much, and some could use a little help. It all depends on the venue you choose. A winery or resort is beautiful and may need little work. A barn, field, or yard may need more. Sometimes it's just extra lighting for a night wedding. You will need sufficient lighting for dining tables and the dance floor, plus other crucial areas. We have worked with some very creative lighting experts over the years.

Fabric and draping can add a dramatic look and soften a big space and create a more intimate setting. This is something that a design company or your florist can provide. We use sheer draping frequently, with or without lighting underneath. Flowers, my biggest love, can enhance the guest tables and transform the altar. Your florist should be able to repurpose flowers to save a little money. Flowers used at the altar can often be moved inside for the tables. A creative florist can enhance any wedding. There is a difference between a full service florist and a florist. The full service florist will deliver, set up, and wait until after the ceremony to repurpose. They can also add to or make additional boutiques or boutonnières on site if needed. A florist that is not full service will drop the flowers, possibly place the flowers, and then leave. So make sure you ask your florist if they're full service. Also give them an approximate budget or price range. If you have a limited flower budget, then possibly use more greenery with fewer flowers.

Candles are also a wonderful touch, and I always recommend five on each dining table. Not tea lights or fake candles, but real candles if your venue will allow it. Candles make any space romantic and soften the room. Most florists will suggest that you purchase your own to keep costs down. Candles should always be dripless so that rented linens are not damaged. I have weddings where the family provided their own candles without being in secure or glassed containers and the linens were ruined by the wax. The rental company billed them for the cost of the linens, which far exceeded the rental price.

I have had some brides or families that insist that they will provide their own flowers and table arrangements. How hard can it be, right? Everyone has a cousin or good friend that has a knack for flowers. They can just go to the flower mart, buy the flowers, and put the arrangements together. Easy peasy, right? Sometimes this has worked in the past, but often not so well.

I remember one wedding where the bride ordered the flowers online and had a work party the day before with her bridal party. She had hired one of my favorite florists to do fabric draping and extra lighting but no flowers. I always ask who is responsible for the delivery of the flowers, and the time they will be arriving to set up. This Saturday, here came six bridesmaids and their spouses or dates carrying in ten huge table arrangements, plus their own homemade bouquets. One look and I knew they were not going to work. They were too large for the tables with the glassware and china already on the tables. They were also loosely done, with flowers hanging over the side. They had also done some arrangements to stand on tall glass pillars. When we tried to place the arrangement on the pillar, the whole thing tipped and would land in the guest's lap, and they would be soaked.

I told the ladies, "Sorry, but these won't work unless we make the arrangements smaller and more secure." I didn't have the time to do this.

The bridesmaids were in tears and they were already late for pre-wedding photos. Thank God the florist who was there hanging the fabric saw my dilemma and offered to help. He could fix this mess in two hours if it was okay with the ladies. No charge since we work together all the time, and he's just a great guy. He had to completely redo every arrangement, and then he started on the bouquets, which were haphazard at best, with loose stems hanging out everywhere. The bride was told before she walked into the reception that the flowers had received professional help, and she was extremely grateful. She later reached out to thank this kind and generous florist.

There is one extremely unprofessional florist that I had the poor luck of working with only twice, thank goodness. His arrangements are basic with not a lot of creativity to them, but my issue with this florist was his attitude. We had gone head to head during the set up. We often have petals down the aisle, and I ask the florist to place those thirty or so minutes before so the photographer can shoot the ceremony site. This florist on both occasions told me no, that he would sprinkle the petals down the aisle himself while the guests were seated. He would be a kind of flower girl.

I just stared at him and said, "Are you kidding me? You are going to walk down the aisle wearing jeans and sprinkle rose petals just before the bride walks?"

"Yes," he said, "I think it's funny, and don't tell me how to do my job."

I told the photographer what the florist had planned, and he replied, "No way in hell is he walking down the aisle in my photos." The photographer was as good as his word, and told our dear florist that he was to spread the petals thirty minutes before as I had instructed so that he could film the ceremony sight. After the ceremony when we were double-checking the room before bringing in the guests, I noticed some large clamp on the bride and groom's Sweetheart table. It was clipped to the front of the table and looked like a vise used in a mechanics' garage.

The photographer and I looked at each other. "What is that thing and why is it on the table?" The florist was standing behind us and smugly informed us that this was for the bride's bouquet to clamp on the table. Normally we lay the bride's bouquet on the table to be part of the centerpiece. The photographer picked the clamp up and threw it across the room. "This stupid thing is not going to ruin my photos." The florist left after that, and hopefully, we will never have to work together again.

I have worked with some wonderful florists over the years doing incredible work. One of those was a gentleman that was at the top of his game about ten years ago. He was number one on many vendor lists. He did a great job was reasonable and pleasant to work with and then something changed. I wasn't sure what it was at first. He started showing up late the day of the wedding, and the flowers didn't look as fresh. He seemed distracted and nervous. I put it down to overbooking for the weekend. Then I started getting phone calls from my brides saying that their credit card had been run two or three times, and he wasn't returning their calls. I finally got in touch with him by phone and asked him what the problem was. He said so sorry. It was a bookkeeping error, and they would make sure the client got a credit.

But more phone calls followed, along with no credits issued and more brides upset. I was very worried; my first obligation is to my couple. Every time I got in touch with him, he gave the same excuse, credit card machine broke, bookkeeping error, etc. The next and last wedding I did with him at one of our regular venues, he arrived very late. He also didn't seem to have enough flowers with him to do the job. The manager of the venue found me putting out place cards and was irate. He had found said florist outside picking flowers from their garden. He was literally making the arrangements from the venue's flowers. He was also scheduled to do fabric draping at the ceremony site, and that wasn't happening. I approached him and asked him what in the hell was going on. I said, "The flowers are not acceptable, you didn't bring any draping, and you are stealing from your clients since none of them had been credited back." He just looked at me in tears, said he couldn't do it anymore, that he had problems. He said he was done and walked out.

Great. Well, the show must go on. I spoke with the bride's mom, told her the story, did not tell the bride, and Jim and I did the best we could with the flowers. We borrowed extra candles from the venue to decorate the tables. For the fabric draping, we knew another florist that stocked draping. We called her, explained the situation, and asked if we could borrow some fabric. After she agreed, Jim drove back to Napa, picked up the fabric, drove back to the venue with one hour to spare, and we hung and draped to the best of our ability. The day went well; obviously the flowers were not as lovely as planned or deserved. The next morning I left a voicemail for the florist, that I would never work with him again, and the venue took him off their referral list.

The bride's mother called me later that week and thanked me. She was suing the florist in small claims court for the money she had paid and never got credit for and the job never completed. She asked me to go to court with her as a witness, which I did. The florist did not show up in court, and after months of going through this mess with the courts, she did not get any money back. I did get in touch with his other brides that I was working with and let them know that they should find another florist. He just disappeared. A year or two later, I did hear from another vendor that he was in drug rehab. I was so sorry for him and those couples that depended on him. Helpful hint: check out your vendors, ask for references, look at their websites, and ask lots of questions. They should be bonded and licensed.

A quick note on flowers: some flowers have a center or stem that can permanently stain clothing. I learned this early on when moving arrangements from one point to another, and I ruined several very nice dresses. I tried dry cleaning and washing—neither worked. I am now told that if you blow it off, not brush, you can remove this powdery substance. The one flower that I remember that does this damage is a Stargazer Lily. Most florists remove the center stem to prevent this damage. Also remember not to place flowers with a heavy scent on the dining tables. Otherwise the scent may overpower the food.

A mother's best friend offered to do the bouquets and boutonnières for the bridal party, while a local florist did the church and table arrangements. At the church the friend handed me the bouquets to pass out and the boutonnières to pin on the gentlemen. The only problem was that the roses were huge and fully open. Not only were they droopy, but they were way too large for the guy's lapels. The stems were so thick that the little pins the friend had supplied would not begin to pierce the fabric of the lapels.

I carry extra pins, but the roses just drooped and looked ridiculous. A couple of the guys said they were not going to wear these stupid flowers and I agreed. So we decided the guys would go without. When the bride's mom arrived at the church, she asked why the guys weren't wearing their flowers. I showed her the sagging boutonnières and told her why we all had agreed to veto them. She agreed that they were a mess and she would speak with her friend. When Mom found her friend and explained how disappointed she was, she said, "I thought you had some talent, but forget that." The friend told Mom where to stick it and she left, never to return for the day.

Many of our weddings will have fresh rose petals down the aisle. They add a beautiful touch and are much nicer than the old cloth or paper runner. Cloth or paper runners are easy to trip on when a heel gets caught. I have seen more than one bride or bridesmaid go down while walking down the aisle. Rose petals can be expensive, but in my opinion they are worth the expense. The bride can use petals in her wedding colors. Be sure to ask you venue if they allow fresh petals. Most churches don't allow them. Amazingly, the bride's dress does not disturb the petals.

We were doing rose petals at one particular outdoor wedding and the florist had just sprinkled them down the aisle. We normally do this within twenty to thirty minutes before the ceremony, and since the petals are down the middle, the guests still have room to walk to their seats. I was chatting with the caterer as I finished placing pillar candles down the aisle when I noticed some of the petals moving. That's odd—there was no wind. So I walked closer to the petals, looked down and Oh my God, there was a snake slithering through the petals. Well, this won't do when the bridal party starts to walk down the aisle. Can you imagine the screams and the mass exit of the ceremony? Okay, we need to move this snake. It looked like a garter snake...not poisonous, at least I didn't think so, but I also didn't give it a second look. Okay florist, move the snake.

"Oh, no," he said. "I'm afraid of snakes!" Well, that makes two of us, but someone has to move that damn snake. One of the catering staff, a tiny young woman, walked over, called us cowards, picked up the poor little snake, and carried him or her out to the lawn area. She told us, "You are both ninnies." She had grown up on a farm and thought snakes were cute. "They handle the vermin, you know." Another crisis averted.

The petals down the aisle remind me of the bride that wanted to have feathers down the aisle. I had never used feathers, and I wasn't sure that they would stay down, but the bride was adamant. The bride is always right, so I said, "Sure. I'm game."

The day of the wedding the bride brought me two large feather pillows, and once I cut open the pillows I would have feathers. What a great idea using pillows instead of me plucking ducks. So I slit the pillows thirty minutes before the ceremony seating and proceeded to spread the feathers down the aisle. But the fluffy feathers didn't want to stay down. A slight breeze combined with the weightlessness of the feathers was not a good combination. Good luck. It's a good thing I had two pillows since they would fly as soon as they hit the ground. When the bridal party walked and then the bride, the feathers flew in all directions except for a few which clung to the ladies' dresses. Overall, it was a mess. The ceremony area looked like a barnyard by the time the ceremony ended.

During the cocktail hour the feathers had to be cleaned up by the venue's staff, and the feathers are impossible to sweep up. Jim jumped in found an old shop vacuum and starting vacuuming. A week later when we did another wedding at the same venue, we were still finding feathers, and after a light rain, they were wet feathers. The venue staff and Jim are still laughing about the feather wedding to this day.

If a couple decides to have a friend or family member provide the décor or flowers, make sure that they know what they're getting into. They need to have the time to deliver and properly do the set up, and make sure they will come back at the end of the night to break down. Too many times family members come drop of the décor or flowers and then say, "Oh, can you finish this? We're late for photos." or something like that. Well, we don't have time either, and we're not always sure how the bride wanted her décor set up. We had one outside evening wedding that needed overhead lighting. The couple did not want to hire a professional lighting team. One of their friends would be bringing the string lighting and hanging it from the trees. No problem. The day of the wedding the friend arrived late, got out his ladder, and proceeded to hang the lighting. The catering staff was setting up tables, and I was putting out table numbers and favors. It was getting late, and the lighting was not even close to being done.

Finally the friend said, "The hell with this. I'm not getting paid, and I need to leave and get to the church. You want it done, you can finish it yourself." He left, and as it was, we would not have enough lighting for guests to eat outside let alone see what they were eating. Jim and one of the catering staff jumped in and finished hanging the lighting, which put everything else behind. Again, crisis averted, but it put all the staff behind. The gentlemen did not even thank us for finishing his job. Hire a professional, and then I can yell at them for not completing their job. With a friend or family member, I can't yell but merely explain that they have an obligation to you. They can then tell me, as that gentleman did, "Lady, go to hell."

Cakes are often another task that a cousin or friend will volunteer for. I'm told that this friend or family member is almost professional and this will save the couple money. "That's fine with me, just remind them that they are responsible for the set up and let them know the time of the set up," . One of my brides asked a good friend to make and deliver her cake. The cake actually looked pretty good, but as she was setting up the cake and putting the cake topper on the cake, it started to slide off its stand. Down the cake went to the floor. Thank God the linen went down with the cake so the cake didn't touch the floor, but it did get flattened on one side and had large bald spots with frosting missing. She burst into tears. Great, here we go again.

The florist was still there. We picked up the cake. The friend smoothed the frosting, the florist stuck flowers in all bald spots, and we turned the cake so it wasn't so noticeable that the cake was a wee bit lopsided. We also covered the stained linen with rose petals so the grease stain didn't show. When finished it looked great, and no one, including the couple, knew that there had been a slight accident. The situation could have been so much worse with the cake dirty and dented.

Wow, speaking of dirty cakes, we had a wedding where a friend who owned a bakery (or so we heard) was going to be making the cake. It was in a town an hour away. The cake was scheduled for delivery at five o'-clock. When it didn't come, I called the number given for the baker and was told while driving down, he had a small fender bender and had to return to the store to fix the cake. Okay, well I had to have the Cake before nine o'clock for the cake cutting. He assured me he would make it. At ten minutes to nine he arrived at the back door to the venue and asked one of the catering staff to help him carry the cake into the kitchen and then to the table for set up. The caterer did help him and then she came to me and told me that I should know that the cake is covered in dog hair.

"What? Are you kidding me?"

"No," she said," I helped him get the cake out of the back of the car where there was a dog bed and dog hair all over the seats." We did the best we could in the kitchen plucking off dog hair before we set it out for cutting. How do you warn your guests to watch for fuzzes as they eat? Do you have the DJ announce, "Dog hair alert, peel off your frosting, or at least pick off the big clumps!" Yuck!

If you do hire a professional, check them out and confirm the delivery day and time at least a week ahead of the scheduled event. I always confirm with my vendors by phone and email in my timeline the day and time. However, just last year, the cake did not arrive at five o'clock. At six, I called the bakery and asked where the cake was. I was told the wedding was the following day and not to worry. I told them, I'm here now and the wedding is today. I reminded the gentlemen on the phone that I had confirmed with my timeline and email.

"Yes," he said, "but I have in my paperwork the wedding is tomorrow, so my paperwork must be right."

"Okay, well you know what you can do with your paperwork, and I want that cake here within one hour. Use the back door so you are not seen." I don't know what he did or whose cake he brought, but we had a cake within the hour. Sometimes, you just have to put your foot down. I also understand why caterers or venues will not be responsible for moving or setting up a cake. It's too easy to damage or mark the cake, let alone drop the cake. Just one time, years ago, I was asked to deliver a small forty-person cake to a venue thirty minutes from home since I was there doing the wedding anyway. It would save them money. No problem, except it was a very hot day. I turned the AC so high that I couldn't feel my feet on the accelerator or brake. With my driving skills, that was not a good thing.

I was worried, and I kept looking over my shoulder at the cake. Once I arrived at the venue, the cake was starting to slide and looked ready to melt. The caterer quickly put it in the freezer, and then, using a knife, tried to prop it up again. By the time it was time to cut the cake, it looked fine, but it was a bit chilly inside. I have never offered to transport a cake again. There was a day that I was forced to help deliver a cake, not necessarily transport it. We were at a private estate up a very steep hill. The baker, well known for his elaborate theme designs, called me on my cell phone and said that he couldn't get up the hill. He asked if I would please meet him at the bottom.

I walked down the driveway. I could see his problem. The driver was alone, and if he drove up the hill, there was no one to hang on to the cake on this sloping driveway. I had two choices: I could drive the van with the stick shift or I could sit in the back with the cake between my legs and hold it steady. You're right, I chose to drive. The cake was an amazing Mad Hatter's cake with the layers already set at a tilted angle. It was beautiful, perfect, and very expensive. We made it, he set it up, and then all we had to do was control the children that came early and continued to race around this amazing cake.

We also have the relatives that insist on bringing the bride and groom's favorite desserts, cookies, or biscotti. We did have this wonderful little lady, the groom's auntie, bring nine dozen homemade biscotti on the plane with her from New Jersey. She said she wanted to surprise the groom with his childhood favorite. I did set them out later by the coffee on a tray that I had borrowed from the venue. Auntie approached me after dinner and asked if I had tried one. No, I had not. I normally don't eat at the weddings. It's not very professional, but, yes, I would try her biscotti.

"Well, what do you think?" she asked after I tried a bite.

"Oh, it's amazing. You must have worked so hard," I replied. Hard was the word; so hard I could not chew it.

At the end of the night, we had eight dozen biscotti still on the table. I do think it's wonderful when a family member contributes something personal like cookies, but I would also suggest that small plastic bags be provided so that the guests can take them home as a favor and not have to eat the cookie on site.

Desserts are now as popular as cakes, maybe even more so. We've had dessert stations with a variety of mini desserts. Also pies, donuts, and s'-mores have become very popular. We have set up many s'more stations with a propane fire pit, and all the ingredients needed for the s'mores: marshmallows, graham crackers, chocolate, and a variety of toppings. We have also had espresso bars brought onto the venue. They are usually a little cart with an attendant that makes the espresso in whatever flavor the guest chooses. One Thanksgiving one very generous bride did individual pies, pumpkin and apple for guest desserts. They were wonderful and about six inches wide and three inches deep. She had ordered two for every guest, and at the end of the night we had forty or so left. The bride and groom lived on the East Coast, so they could not take the leftovers, nor could their guests. She asked me to distribute them amongst the catering staff. I did, and Jim and I ended up with fifteen. I didn't need to buy pies that year for the holiday. This is one of the perks of our business, leftover desserts and flowers. I can't stand to throw these goodies in the trash. I normally pass out the desserts and cake to the staff; we don't need the calories. A flower arrangement is always welcome in our house. We will frequently donate the leftover flowers to local hospitals and nursing homes.

Flowers bring joy to everyone, male or female. We have found that police officers and couples in law enforcement tend to enjoy donuts as treats at the end of the night. We had one couple with the CIA order late night hamburgers from a local drive thru. I guess it's true; law enforcement has to eat on the run and frequents the drive-thrus.

When ordering cakes or desserts, you need to keep in mind food allergies, gluten, nuts, etc. We did one wedding that could have been disastrous, and almost was. We were at a private resort in the Valley, and the bride and groom had ordered two cakes, one larger white cake, and a smaller chocolate peanut butter cake. Both were beautiful and yummy. Both cakes had signage in front that displayed the flavors so that guests could choose once the cakes were cut. There were also printed menus at the dining tables listing the meal choices and the cake flavors. All guests should have been aware. However, one lady, a relative of the bride, chose to try a bit of both cakes. The evening was winding down and the bride and groom were saying goodnight to their guests when this lady started yelling that she couldn't breathe. Okay, I was not going to panic, and I called 911. The paramedics were there in under ten minutes and transported her to the closest up-valley hospital. The paramedics had told me it looked like anaphylactic shock. The bride and groom had already gone back to their room. I didn't want to disturb them, so I went to the bride's mother's room and told her that I thought she should go to the hospital since she was a relative.

Jim drove up as the ambulance was leaving. He had been doing a wedding just down the road with one of our assistant coordinators. He wanted to know what I had done this time. I was worried sick all night about this woman. The next morning I got a call from the lady's husband that his wife had almost died because she's allergic to peanuts, and he was going to sue me, the resort, the caterer, and the cake provider. He then proceeded to call each of these vendors. I spoke to each of the vendors who were terribly upset by this woman's trauma and none of us could afford to be sued, financially or reputation wise.

About two hours later the bride's mother called me and told me that she had spent all night at the hospital and had also spoken to other relatives that were sitting at the same table with the lady who ate the peanut butter cake. She told them she knew she was allergic to peanuts but the cake looked so good that she didn't think a little bit would hurt her. The bride's mother assured me no one was going to be sued, since the lady knew full well that she was putting herself at risk by eating the cake. Apologies were made and that was the end of that.

Good rule to go by: ask your guests for any possible allergies on the response cards. Label desserts and cakes, especially if they have ingredients that contain nuts or ingredients that could cause an allergic response. On my timelines I always list the guest's names, table numbers, and guests that have allergies. The caterers also get a list of guests with allergies. So thank goodness, we have never had another issue like the peanut butter cake.

Chapter 10:

Ministers for Life

I BECAME A LICENSED MINISTER twenty-two years ago, and Jim followed, getting licensed two years later. We do so many weddings at private venues, estates, wineries, and hotels now and fewer weddings at churches. Most of our weddings are destination weddings with our couples coming from all over the world. And many of these weddings are not in churches. I had worked for years with a local friend and lawyer that was a licensed minister and would travel with me to any location needed. When he decided to retire to Hawaii, he came to see me at the store and told me it was time for me to take over the mantle. He sent in the paperwork for me, and two weeks later I was licensed. Wow, I was official, should I wear robes or a nice suit? Who would hire me? Yes, I was already doing weddings, but did my brides know that I was now a member of the clergy?

My first wedding was for a dear friend getting remarried. He asked that I officiate for his small, backyard family wedding. Yes, I would be honored. Should I mention that his ex-wife is also a good friend? No, let the ex-husband tell her. Not my problem. So I wrote up the vows and prepared for my debut. My biggest concern that day would be not to call the new bride by the old wife's name. All I can remember thinking is, *Her name is Sue, it's John and Sue, John and Sue.* The wedding went fine, and they are still together to this day. However, two days later, his ex-wife called me. "How could you do this to me? You should have told me." She eventually did forgive me, and yes, she remarried, and no, she did not ask me to officiate.

I continued to do officiating to polish my skill set, gaining confidence as I went. I started small, doing weddings for the brides that I had met at my store. They knew me and yes, I was cheaper than other officiants or ministers. My earlier weddings were for the customers and friends.

I did a wedding for the neighbor that used to help me with my catering. He met this wonderful woman during a night of line dancing, right after I met Jim, and they asked me to perform the ceremony. It was a country western theme, of course. It was in their new home, and we all wore western clothes and cowboy boots. It was so fun and very nostalgic. They cried, I cried. I told stories of how often he had come to my house to commiserate, help cut fruit, and eat most of it, and just being a good friend and neighbor for twenty-four years. I love the ceremonies that you can ad-lib and speak from the heart.

Another wedding I also did for friends was a rock and roll wedding. This wedding was in their backyard for one hundred or so guests. The four attendants and I walked out to sixties music. One of the bridesmaids sang a very fun rock and roll song, while the rest of us swayed and sang back up. It was so fun, and I still see these couples today.

After these easier weddings, I felt I was ready for the big time. I did several weddings in a church. That was scary, and I got so nervous once that I asked all the guests to rise, and I forgot to tell them to sit back down. They stood for one hour during the wedding. The church was very gracious to let me use their wonderful venue. The bride wanted something untraditional in a traditional setting, if that makes sense.

I did a wedding a year or so ago where the bride and groom spoke very little English and the guests not at all. When I walked in first to stand at the altar, all the guests clapped, and I thought wow, I must look great, or they're happy to see me. Then when the bridal party and the bride and groom walked in, they also clapped, so then I realized it was the custom… not just me. Damn, and I thought it was my new suit or the great haircut.

I have done weddings in very strange and challenging places. One wedding I did was rather unnerving. It was held on a cliff overlooking the ocean in Muir Woods on the Northern Coast. We stood on a rocky ledge facing out to the sea. When all the guests were on the ledge with the bride, groom, and me, it was getting very tight, and I had to keep backing up. I was maybe two feet from the edge of going over the cliff; the wind was howling, the fog was rolling in, and it was freezing. The waves were lapping up so high that the three of us could feel the water on the back of our legs. Halfway through the ceremony, the groom leaned over and said, "Hurry up and cut it short. I'm afraid we're going to tumble into the ocean." So I did. I have to admit it was a wee bit scary and a lot cold.

The next two weddings were also scary. I got a call from a photographer that I had worked with for years, and he was also the photographer for one of the big hot air balloon companies in the Valley. Hot air balloon rides are very big in our little community. This photographer called and asked if I could officiate for two weddings in a hot air balloon, one on Friday and one the following Monday. The officiant that they normally used had broken his arm—not flying, thank God.

"Sure," I said. "I should mention that I have never been up in a balloon before, and I'm not a good flyer." When I fly commercial I normally drink Bloody Marys or wine. But to get the chance to fly for free and get paid, plus a champagne breakfast after, well, I couldn't turn it down.

Balloons fly at six in the morning before the wind comes up, so I had to be at the launch area by half past five. The first wedding in the balloon was the couple, the pilot, one witness, the photographer, and I. These balloon baskets come in various sizes and some can hold up to sixteen people. The pilot asked Jim if he wanted to go along, no charge, but Jim, like me, is not a good flyer, so he declined. We took off, and I have to say it was wonderful. It's like floating and not like flying. You fly lower, at less than three thousand feet, and you can see the cars, the houses, the cattle

grazing; it was great. Once we were at a decent height, the pilot said I could start.

In order to hold my book, and stand upright, I looped my arm around one of the ropes on the side of the basket. The ceremony went well, and I took my time. When the pilot had to add air, it is a loud *swoosh*ing sound, so I would say, "Do you," *swoosh*, "take her as your wife?" *swoosh*. So the ceremony took longer than it normally would. When finished, we had time to enjoy the scenery below, and the photographer got some great photos.

We landed about two hours later with a small thud when we hit the ground. Piece of cake. I was ready for the next one on Monday.

Monday's wedding was a bit different. It was foggy in our Valley that morning, so we drove forty-five minutes or so to another county where the sun was shining and we were able to launch. Jim followed us up in our car. The basket was smaller this time with just the couple, the pilot, and me. The photographer got pictures from the ground before and after the ceremony. It was windier that day and the pilot told us it could be rougher. Oh joy, such fun. The groom also wanted to include his family in the ceremony, so he had his phone on with his family all listening in on the ceremony. Okay, Darlene, no swearing. We took off and continued to climb to a calmer elevation.

I started the ceremony, all good, and then the pilot said, "We're drifting into that mountain. I'm going to try to climb above it, so hang on it may get rough."

"Okay, do you," *swoosh*, "take her…" *swoosh*. You get the picture. When the ceremony was finished, the pilot had some fun by flying low and scaring cows and watching them run. The landing was rougher than Friday, and we had to jump out quickly to help hold the balloon down since the chase crew hadn't arrived yet. It was fun, and I would definitely do it again. I had to ask the pilot what county we were in in order to sign the license. I wasn't sure since we had traveled between three counties in our flight. I let the pilot be the witness and also determine the county, at least the best he could, of where we were when I said, "I now pronounce you husband and wife."

One wedding I did was in an old mission. The bride and groom forgot the wedding rings at home an hour away. They insisted that the guests enjoy the bar and appetizers until the best man returned with the rings. He forgot the key to the house and had to break a window to get in and retrieve the rings. By the time the rings arrived, most of the guests were past caring and half of the guests had left. After the ceremony, there were no appetizers for the cocktail hour. All in all, it was quite a day. So couples, remember: make a list! Without the license the ceremony is not legal.

This reminds me of another wedding that I did in a small resort poolside. I woke up with laryngitis. I felt okay but I could barely be heard. A mic was also not provided to me. Since it was a small wedding of sixty people, the bride and I thought I could most likely be heard, but not that day. Before the ceremony, I asked for the license.

"Oh, it's in the car, we'll give it to you afterward," the bride said. We got through the ceremony with the guests trying to read my lips. After the ceremony I again asked for the license so I could go home. The groom proceeded to tell me that they didn't have a license yet, that his divorce had just become final the day before and they hadn't gotten a license yet. I explained that they were not legally married, but if they could bring me the license in the next day or two, I could do the ceremony anywhere with just the two of them and a witness, sign the license, and it would be legal. That is what we did two days later, honeymoon delayed. In California the marriage license has to be obtained within ninety days before the ceremony, and anywhere within the state of California.

Jim also had a wedding for two FBI agents that were scheduled to be married in June at a local winery. In February the couple was transferred to the LA branch. But in order to be sent together, they had to be married. So Jim met them at the local county recorder's office, performed the ceremony outside in the rain, and I was the witness. We then signed the license, Jim took it back inside, and bam, it's legal and they could both go to LA. They had the wedding for their guests in June with none of the guests any the wiser.

Sometimes the couples don't understand the meaning of "within ninety days before the ceremony." We have this written in our instructions and tell them, but sometimes, they just don't get it. They show up, no license, and expect Jim or I to still do the ceremony. We have to explain this ceremony won't be legal and they must get a license. In most all cases, they get a license the next day or Monday, we meet them repeat a quick ceremony, and then it's legal. The license will not bear the date of the ceremony with your guests in attendance.

I have officiated maybe seventy or so weddings over the years, but not as many as Jim has done. I can either coordinate or officiate, but not both.

Jim has become so good at it, professional and yet humorous, with lots of emotion. He said he enjoys being so close to the couple that he feels their love and emotions. Once he started working with me on officiating, we decided to call this part of our business, "Memorable Moments," since it is a life-changing day. We now advertise the business under this name and also on our website.

Jim has done all kinds of weddings and ceremonies: Wine, Sand, Hand, and Unity Candles ceremonies. He had done wedding for all denominations. We both have learned so much about different cultures and religions. One wedding that Jim did that stands out in my memory was a lovely couple that were doing an Indian wedding in a church and then the reception in a winery. The priest was coming over from India and the wedding was in a local church. I was at the rehearsal the night before when the bride's sister told me that the priest was not sure he was licensed for the US and I should have Jim at the church in the morning just in case. So that night I told Jim to wear a suit and be at the church with me by nine o'clock in the morning. The reception would be that night at six o'clock. The coordinator at the church was new, so I was going to get everyone down the aisle. However, more family than planned showed up to be in the procession, and then to be seated. These family members did not speak English, so communications aside, I just lined everyone up and then just motioned *you go, then you, then you,* until I ran out of family. Some days you just have to wing it.

The priest did not speak any English, so yes, Jim was in. Jim and the priest went up the aisle, then the groom and then bridal party and bride. Of course, Jim did not understand what he was supposed to do and he couldn't understand what was being said. The bride's sister said she would cue him. So after twenty minutes the priest stopped talking, and the sister looked at Jim, and then not knowing what part he was to play, he said a few of the words that he normally uses to close a wedding, pronounced them, and they all walked out. Jim signed the license, and no one would ever know that the bride, groom, priest, and Jim were flying by the seat of their pants. You do whatever it takes to get through it.

One wedding Jim did was to be the assistant to the officiant. The officiant, a friend of the bride and groom and also a psychiatrist, was ninety-three years old. The couple wanted to honor him but wasn't sure he was up to the task, so they asked Jim to be at the altar with the doctor and to sign the license.

It was going well, but the doctor would say a few words and then forget where he was in the ceremony and pronounce them husband and wife. Jim would tap him on the shoulder and mention that the couple had not yet done their vows. He would do the vows, and then he was ready to pronounce them again when Jim tapped his shoulder again. It was time for the rings. Everyone laughed, including the doctor, and the ceremony ended. We are always available to do stand up.

Jim and I have both jumped in at the last minute if the officiant or minister didn't show up or was not up to the job. One day Jim got a call from another coordinator that the officiant hired had not shown up. They asked Jim if he was available and how quickly he could get there. He put on a suit, printed up a standard ceremony, and we had another happy couple. Jim and I have both traveled to various locations for ceremonies and are glad to do it. We get a mini vacation and the couples get the ceremony and the location that they wanted. It's important to have a bond and a good relationship with your officiant or minister.

One particular wedding Jim does not remember fondly was that the groom and his groomsmen got drunk before the wedding. They arrived early for photos and it was obvious they had been drinking a good bit before they arrived. They then continued to drink wine before the ceremony. When it was time to walk down the aisle, the groom had red wine stains down his shirt, and the groomsmen had lost their boutonnières and had difficulty walking. During the ceremony, the groom continued to be somewhat unstable on his feet, and Jim kept trying to prop him up and keep him on his feet.

When we got to the dinner the groom was gone—body intact, but consciousness gone.

One of the groomsmen came to me around nine o'clock and said the groom's face was lying in his plate. We had a limo outside to take the couple at the end of the night. I got three groomsmen to carry the groom to the limo and take him back to the hotel. The bride was in tears, and he had literally ruined their big day. This is another one that I wondered if it would last.

We have had grooms throw up and brides faint and have to sit during the ceremony. We always have a chair standing by and smelling salts. Just last year one of my brides was spotted barfing in the trash can outside of the dining area. I normally let Jim hose down and clean up these areas, and believe me, he has done this more than once. He's afraid if I clean it up, I will also be barfing.

We also got our youngest daughter, Rhonda, licensed. She was asked to do some family member weddings, so we helped her get her license and provided her with some sample ceremonies. She added her own personal touches to fit her style. I think she's done four weddings by now. She is a full time hospital administrator, so she really doesn't have time for this job, as fun as it may be.

At one of the family weddings she was doing, Rhonda noticed that the groom's mother's dress was almost transparent in the sunlight, and her panties were visible. Rhonda mentioned,

"Have you never heard of Spanx?" Oh what, the hell? Rhonda went in the bathroom, peeled off her Spanx, and gave them to the groom's mom. Disaster diverted, and you do what you gotta do. I have given my sandals to the bride when her feet gave out. I have shared my sweaters and coats with moms and bridesmaids. I travel with at least two pairs of black shoes and two black sweaters. I have also lost three pairs of black sandals and two black sweaters to forgetful brides.

We have had the privilege to work some amazing professionals over the years. There is a priest that I have worked with for the last fifteen years. He is a joy to work with, kind, professional, and a good friend. There are also several rabbis that I prefer to work with. Couples should put together the ceremony that they want. There is no right or wrong way as long as vows and rings are exchanged. We have learned so much from our couples in various customs and traditions.

One of our couples wanted a priest for their ceremony, and I had re-ferred three priests that I frequently work with and have great respect for. I brought up their websites during our meeting so that the couple could see the pictures and profiles on each of these priests. One of these priests is a lovely older gentleman, but when the bride saw his picture she told the groom, "I'm not working with him. He's as old as dirt, and I don't want a dirty old man doing my wedding."

Excuse me? I told Jim later, "I don't think I can work with a bride that is so rude and so arrogant. Did she think we were as old as dirt?" Would all of her guests be young, including her grandparents, or were they not to be invited because they're old too? Is rudeness hereditary? I certainly hope not. I did do her wedding. I never did warm up to her, but she was too self-absorbed to notice.

I remember one wedding we did with another minister who has a very flamboyant and fun personality. At the rehearsal we went over the procession. The bride was being escorted down the aisle by her mother. I normally ask the bride and her mother or father to hug the bride as they pass the bride off to the groom at the altar. This bride said, "I am not a hugger, and I also don't want any laughing, smiling, or emotion during the ceremony. So keep it straight."

The poor minister was not sure he could do it. He normally cracks jokes, gives the couple hugs and just has a good time. He got through it with a straight face, but it was not a very fun day for those involved. I wonder how long that marriage lasted. I think between Jim and I, we'd done close to six hundred weddings. Each ceremony is different and wonderful in its own way. Well, almost every one of them is wonderful. We still get Christmas cards from many of our couples. We like to say, "The couples we put together stay together."

Chapter 11:

Animals and Weddings

*I*T HAS BECOME VERY POPULAR THE LAST FEW YEARS to have animals in weddings. Most venues and wineries are animal and dog friendly. Animals are like family members and should be part of your wedding if you choose. Just remember to bring food for them and a portable bed or blanket for them if they are going to stay through the entire evening.

The first wedding I did with a dog was about eleven years ago. This was at a very elegant country club in Napa. The dog, a German Shepherd, was also the ring bearer with the actual ring on a collar on his neck. He did well at the rehearsal, but the day of the wedding, he saw all these people, got spooked, and turned and ran down the fairway. Stop that dog! Oh hell, I was not going chase that big dog, forget it. He was eventually caught, but no longer had the job of Ring Dog. We were lucky to get the rings back. Reminder, don't put the real rings on the dog. Use fake rings with the real rings in the best man's pocket.

Another wedding with a dog, and another German Shepherd, this time with bad hips. The dog was fifteen years old and had hip dysplasia as many larger dogs do. The bride adored this dog and he had to be in her wedding. The bride's sister said if the dog couldn't make it down the stairs to the altar, she would carry him. The dog also had cancer with just weeks to live. I met this poor fellow at the rehearsal. He had straps on his hips with a leash to hold his hips up and take weight off his legs. I very seldom cry at weddings, but I sobbed through the rehearsal. The next day at the wedding, the poor fellow could not make it down the stairs. The tiny little bridesmaid and sister picked up the dog and carried him down the stairs to the altar. Not only was I sobbing, but so were all the guests and the bride.

During dinner and the reception the dog was set up on a very nice bed next to the bride and Groom's Sweetheart table. Everyone was in love with that dog. The caterers brought him food, water, and none of us could walk by without bending over to give him a pat or hug.

One summer wedding we had a large dog, a Great Pyrenees, who was the ring dog. This long-haired, very large dog suffers from overheating. The dog made it down the aisle and lay on Jim's feet while he was offici-ating. Jim had to stop the ceremony several times for water breaks for the dog. It was a hot day, and the groom was concerned that the dog was over-heating. We stopped while we got a bowl of water and let the dog cool off before continuing. At the end of the ceremony, the prostrated dog was car-ried out by one of the groomsmen. We took him inside during the cocktail hour to keep him out of the heat. Whether man or beast, they must be treated with love and sometimes support. I truly believe all animals go to heaven. I hope to meet a few of my buddies there.

We have done maybe forty weddings with dogs; some in suits, some wearing bow ties, and some wearing flowered collars. I'm not sure the dog enjoys it, but they are family, after all. One couple had a small pug, who also happened to have only weeks to live with cancer and was carried in and out. Again, here come the tears.

We had a wedding last year where the little dog came for the ceremony but not the reception. The dog suffered from a nervous condition and hated crowds, so the bride asked Jim to take the dog back to the hotel about ten minutes away. The minute the dog got to the altar, it was handed to Jim and off they went to the hotel. Jim said the dog cuddled up to him in the car with his head under his arm. Jim settled him at the hotel room with food and water, and then returned to help me with the wedding. We fill the roles we are given.

At another wedding we had a falcon. This falcon with the rings attached to him was to fly from his trainer to the groom at the altar. The trainer was out of sight and the groom had a leather band on his arm to protect his arm. It was amazing to see, and it happened so quickly. One minute the bird was on the trainer's arm, the next it was flying over my head to the groom's arm. It was beautiful, if not a bit daunting. The trainer had actually brought two birds in case one did not perform. She brought them in cages and explained that they are hunters and never a pet and can always be dangerous.

We then had the horse. Not a horse and carriage, but a groom arriving on horseback. This is common during an Indian wedding, called the Baraat, or the groom's procession. You can also use an elephant, but the cost for the elephant was ten thousand dollars and had to be brought up from LA, so we used a horse instead. The horse was still expensive but less so than the elephant. The venue was a winery and everyone would enter on a private road with a drummer, bridal party, family, photographer, and the groom on the horse. The horse was beautifully decorated, as was our groom. The horse was very well trained; with the loudness of the drum, I would certainly hope so. Any other horse would have bolted. The groom said he's not fond of horses but he was willing, and it is tradition. I have to say this was one of my favorite weddings. The bride looked stunning in her beautiful gown, and the glorious colors of reds and purples were worn by both the men and the women. The bride changed gowns several times throughout the day-long event. The family was wonderful to work with, and I can't wait to do the bride's sister's wedding.

Chapter 12:

Caterers, or So They Say

MANY VENUES, RESORTS, HOTELS, AND WINERIES provide their own in-house caterer. However, some of these venues don't provide these services but have a good referral list of excellent professional caterers. Some of our couples have chosen to bring in the caterer of their choice. Some of these caterers are chefs, or are small, private restaurant owners, or even the casual BBQ shack. Even though the food may be excellent and just what the couple enjoys, they may not be prepared to handle a larger event or wedding.

One wedding we did about six years ago was at a beautiful winery up the coast, two and a half hours from our home in Napa. We had been referred by another bride in New York. Jim and I agreed to meet with the bride and groom at the winery six months before the wedding to go over the details. The winery had very clear rules of the timing, use of the property, and hours. The Bride wanted to use her choice of caterers and selected a chef from a restaurant in San Francisco. She had eaten at the restaurant and enjoyed their food. She assured the winery that the chef could provide the staffing and follow all the rules. This chef was not at the meeting but would communicate by phone and email. The winery did not provide the tables, chairs, linens, china, or glassware, so I volunteered to order all the rentals. The ceremony and cocktail hour would be outside in the garden and dinner and dancing in a barn enclosure, which was rustic and lovely.

Over the next few months, I put together a diagram of the ceremony site and the table set up for the barn. The bride wanted rectangular tables to seat eight and a Sweetheart table for the two of them. I placed the rental order with a local rental company I frequently work with for eight by forty rectangular Queen's tables for the guests and a forty-eight inch round for the Sweetheart table. I also ordered the linens, glassware, China, and everything else. I sent a copy to the couple, the caterer, and the winery manager, and asked the couple to make the deposit. A bartending service was hired out of the Bay Area to serve the wine and beer. One set of chairs were ordered and these chairs would be moved from the ceremony site during the cocktail hour to the barn for dinner service. Since the ceremony site was five hundred or so feet away from the barn, the chairs would need to be moved by pickup truck. I would have rented two sets of chairs, but the couple insisted that their groomsmen would stack and transport the chairs from the one area to another.

I had several phone conversations with the chef since we had yet to meet, but he assured me that he was bringing enough staff to set up, cook, serve, and clean up, no problem. The event manager at the winery had some concerns about this—they normally used a caterer that they were familiar with and who knew the property. I was also a little concerned since I had never met this chef, but the bride was insistent all would be fine. The day before the wedding, the rehearsal went well and the bridal party was in good spirits. The wedding was several hours from our home, and Jim and I decided to book a hotel room for the night so we wouldn't have to drive back and forth late at night.

The next day, wedding day, Jim and I arrived at the winery early to oversee the rental deliveries. As the rectangular tables were being set up in the barn, I noticed that they were the wrong size. Instead of Queen's tables, eight by forty, they were eight by thirty, which is much narrower. These are not wide enough to seat eight guests, four on each side, and still have room for the china and glassware, let alone flowers in the center.

I quickly reviewed the rental order that I had placed, and this was not right. I called the rental company and was told that the rental order had been changed the week before by the caterer to possibly save money. The savings is two dollars per table. The linens were okay, just a bit big for the smaller tables. The wine glasses had also been reduced to only one glass for either red or white wine, and not a separate glass for each. There were not enough glasses for the bar and the dining since the count had been reduced. What the hell! All we could do now was adapt. We finished our set up at the ceremony site and oversaw the flower set up with the florist. The two bartenders arrived and set up the wine and beer bar in the barn and a smaller set up in the garden area for the cocktail hour. I suggested to them since the glassware order had been cut to keep all glasses at the bar, and the guests would have to come to the bar for their wine or beer during dinner. There also was not room on the table for glassware since the table size had been reduced.

The caterer/chef arrived with two assistants and started to unload and set up food preparation in the kitchen. I went into the kitchen and asked when the other staff was arriving.

He replied, "What other staff? This is it."

By then, I was boiling mad. "You have a hundred and twenty guests, and you are doing this with two people who are improperly dressed in jeans! And why did you change my rental order?" I asked, which came out more of a growl.

He said, "I thought I'd save the couple a few bucks, and they were grateful."

Yeah, he did it so he might get a bigger tip. At this point there was nothing else to do but go forward and hope for the best. Why don't people ever listen?

The ceremony went off fine. The groomsmen loaded the back of the pickup truck with the chairs, and Jim showed them where to unload in the barn. Then Jim placed them at the tables according to our layout. The two ladies from the bartending service were great but dismayed with the lack of glasses. They would remind the guests to hang on to their glass since we didn't have a backup of extra glasses as we normally do. This, by the way, is so tacky. To ask your guest to hang onto one glass all night, from the cocktail hour, to the table, to the bathroom, back to the table, is just ridiculous. We suggest two and a half times the number of wine glasses per guest for the cocktail hour and then the correct number of glasses with a few extra to be placed at each place setting for dinner service. Normally this is a red, white, a water glass, and a flute for a sparkling if the bride and groom choose to serve Champagne or sparkling.

When it was time for dinner, we invited the guests into the barn for dinner service. The DJ invited guests to be seated and announced if the guests wanted wine they would need to go to the bar set up inside. The bride and groom entered and were seated. I served the bride and groom wine at their table. Dinner was a buffet, and the two helpers were hustling back and forth to get the meal out. We invited the bride and groom first and then the guests to go through the buffet. Refill service of the platters was very slow; the two gentlemen couldn't seem to catch up. Guests were asking for their water to be refilled since it was very warn in the barn. When the guests were coming to me asking for water, I again ventured into the kitchen and asked the chef to have his guys pour water at the tables.

He handed me two water pitchers and he said, "If you want it, pour it yourself. There's a hose outside, and I'm busy."

Great, besides being slow, the caterer is also rude. I handed Jim a pitcher and out we went to pour warm hose water into pitcher and then pass to the guests. This went on for thirty minutes or so, with many trips to the hose.

The winery manager was watching this fiasco in horror. "Never again, never again," she kept muttering. The bar girls were swamped, pouring wine and trying to cool off the guests. When the guests were almost finished eating, I asked the chef if he was providing vendor meals as is standard.

He said, "Nope, they didn't pay for it." So I sent Jim into the nearest town twenty minutes away to pick up pizza for the two bartenders, winery manager, DJ, photographer, and Jim and myself. We found a quiet place outside to eat in shifts during guest dancing. The rest of the evening went off okay until the end of the evening when it was time for breakdown. The winery requested that all the linens be bagged, chairs stacked, kitchen cleaned, floors swept, and ready for the next day. I approached the "chef" and his staff to start the break down.

He said, "We don't do that. We cook, period."

So Jim and I, with the help of the event manager, the two bar girls, a few of the bridal party, pulled and stacked. I drew the line at sweeping and mopping. I was done. The bartender gave me a hug and a bottle of wine for service beyond the call of duty. When I spoke with the bride's family as we were leaving, the bride's brother was mopping. The bride's mother said, "We were told he was a very good chef, and he had promised to provide enough staff." We later learned that he was not the restaurant's head chef, but a line cook in the restaurant.

Another one of these hire-your-own-chef weddings was about three years ago at a small inn up Valley in the late fall. I had been referred by another local bride. We met with the bride and family at the location, which was beautiful. We went over the set up for the outside ceremony and then the cocktail and dinner inside the inn. This would be done on two levels, cocktail hour downstairs and dinner upstairs. It was not a huge room but would work with two rows of long tables put together to form one long table for fifty at each table. When we use long tables, we ask that the couple do assigned seating with the place cards at each guest's place setting and a seating chart to guide guests to their table.

We met with the chef who was from a local restaurant and assured me that sufficient staff would be provided. The bride hired a small band that I had worked with in the past, as well as a local photographer, so we were all set. I always ask for the seating chart a week in advance and then get the place cards the day before. That way, Jim and I can get in early and place the cards, oversee flower and other set ups, and be ready when the bridal party arrives on site. At the rehearsal the bride still had not given me the final set up, place cards, or who was sitting next to whom but assured me I would have it first thing the next morning. However, the next morning, I did not have the seating chart. Tables were set up, linens on, and glassware and flatware on the table. The bride and groom were going to be seated at the middle long table, but that's all we knew at this point.

When the bride arrived at the inn, I told her I had to have a seating chart. I had no idea who was family, who was not, and where she wanted the guests to sit. She gave me a partial list of family and friends and where she thought she might want them, but sorry, she hadn't had time to do the chart, and now she was late for photos. We would just have to figure it out.

"Okay," I told her, "but don't get upset if your guests are not where you want them." Jim and I knew the names of the parents, so everyone with their last name went at a table close to the bride and groom, and the same with the groom's family. The rest was pot luck. Well, our luck may have been in the pot because it started to rain during the ceremony under the trees. The officiant did speed things up the best he could, and we invited everyone inside for the cocktail hour.

Jim and I went back upstairs to continue to do the best we could with the place settings. I worked out the timing with the band and how to announce the bridal party, toasts, etc. After a fifty-minute cocktail hour we invited the guests to look at the tables to find their place card. There was no seating chart to guide guests to their table, since the bride had never completed this, so the seating took longer with guests walking around looking for their names. One lady came to me and said that her table seating can't be right since she and her children were not seated at the same table, and her husband and children were from another country did not speak English. They needed to sit together. It turned out she and her husband had different last names, which is why I didn't know to place them together. I moved them together at one table, then had to change the other place cards until I was moving many couples. The complaints kept coming and I couldn't say, "Well, the bride didn't do the seating chart," so I just kept apologizing. We finally got everyone seated for dinner, which took thirty minutes longer than it should have. Jim came over to ask if I was okay, since I was starting to roll my eyes. Yes, I am a big eye roller.

"Just great, thank you. This is a f—ing mess. Why can't people just do what we ask? I just may quit after today." I actually threaten to quit four or five times a year.

I had gone into the kitchen often to apologize, explain the situation, and keep them updated. They had provided enough staff and servers, so I felt good about this part of the evening. The band announced the bride and groom, and the welcome toast was done by the bride's father. The first course of salad came out and all was going smoothly. We had the first round of toasts, and when the band didn't announce one family member scheduled for toasting, the bride's grandmother came up to the mic and said, "I'm taking over and making the announcements, it's obviously beyond the band's capability." She proceeded to tell stories, some not so appropriate, but the bride and groom didn't seem to mind, so I didn't try to stop her.

Eight children who were guests were in another room of the inn with babysitters. Meals for these children were to be served in that room. The mother that had approached me earlier came to me and asked when the children were going to be fed. Her children didn't speak English and she had been running back and forth between the two areas to check on the children. Both of us thought the children should have been served first. I went into the kitchen and asked the chef when the children would be fed. He was told that a family member had arranged for pizza to be delivered and the chef had not planned a meal for the kids. He could get one out, but it would have to be after the main course was plated and served.

The grandmother was just finishing her toast and came to me to ask about the children's meal. I told her what the chef had said and that he would feed the children as soon as the main course was plated. He would make chicken tenders and mac and cheese.

Well, Grandma was furious. "Take me to the kitchen! I want to talk to that f—ing Chef!" I followed her in and wow, I thought only sailors spoke that way. She told the chef to get the f—-ing meal out to the children NOW and not after the adults. She didn't care whose fault it was, but dammit those kids needed to be taken care of. As we walked out, she asked me, "Where did you find that idiot?" In all honesty, it was not the chef's fault.

The children were fed, the rest of the evening went well, and everyone had a good time. The bride and groom were never aware of the chaos that had transpired, which is always our goal. It's important that all vendors be on the same page, and the bride and groom communicate all their plans to the vendors and the coordinator. Why was I surprised that we had another night of surprises?

∞

I am always wary of working with caterers that I have not worked with before and especially chefs or small diner owners, BBQ places, friends of the family, or food trucks. Some of these have turned out beautifully, but some have been near disasters. Most of the time it comes down to insufficient staffing. You can have an amazing cook, but if you don't have the staff to back him up, it's a terrible waste of talent. I believe the biggest reason couples do this is to save money and perhaps help or please a family member or friend by giving them the job.

One wedding we did at a local winery, our couple insisted on having their friend that owned a small diner provide the meal. We met with the family and caterers and they assured me they could handle it. They were glad to let me handle the rentals, chairs, tables, china, etc. Dinner would be a buffet since less staff is needed. I told them how many staff I thought they needed for meal service and wine service during the evening.

The day of the wedding, the rentals were delivered, the tables were in place, and we were ready to go. The caterer/friend had hired staffing for set up, wine service, etc. When they started dropping or placing the linens, it became clear that they were not professional. They did not know how to place the linens, nor how to fold napkins. So I showed them how to fold the napkins and place the glassware. Appetizers were stationary during the cocktail hour, which would require less staff. One of my biggest peeves is when the linens that don't touch the floor and the use of paper products, whether it is napkins or plates. If it's an outside picnic wedding, that's one thing, but please don't use paper inside at a beautiful venue.

Guests were invited inside for dinner and wine was poured, so far so good. The buffet tables were set up on the dance floor and would be removed immediately after dinner service. The food came out and guests were invited through the buffet. Since we had one hundred and fifty guests, it was suggested by the winery wedding manager and myself that the buffet be open on both sides for guests to make the meal service flow faster. One staff member would oversee replenishing.

The photographer asked me if she and her assistant would receive a vendor meal since it is included in their contract. I spoke with the catering manager and asked about vendor meals. She told me that if there was food left, fine. If not, too bad.

I said, "Well, let me know. If not, I'll ask Jim to pick up pizzas for the vendors." The local pizza joint was due to close in fifteen minutes, and Jim would need to leave soon in order to make it on time. She wasn't happy with me and told me she'd just have to see. I told

Jim he better go get pizza. Jim and I will always take care of our vendors, and yes, we eat too much pizza.

A few minutes later, the bride's grandmother came to tell me that by the time her table got to the buffet, there was no meat of any kind left, only salad and potatoes. She was not a happy guest. I told her I would check with the kitchen. When I spoke with the catering manager again (by now she can't stand the sight of me) I asked her if they had more meat of any kind left in the kitchen. She said no, and it was my fault and the wineries fault that we suggested a two-sided buffet, which made her run out of food faster. Well that didn't make sense. The same amount of food would still be consumed, just faster service. She then screamed at me that we had set her up for failure, and we were just used to fancy caterers. At the end of the night, she just disappeared and left the hired staff to clean up. I don't seem to be making any new friends.

You would think I would give up on these outside caterers, but we have to support our couples and give them what they want, offering the best advice possible. I always set up a meeting with couple and the caterers to go over staffing and expectations. I am more than glad to handle the rentals so that I know we will have enough glassware, etc. A few times I have hired extra bartenders or staffing for these weddings if the caterer cannot provide them.

One of these smaller caterers almost set the winery kitchen on fire. The kitchen is very small with an oven, stovetop, refrigerator, freezer, and a table for work space. During the cocktail hour I heard a shrill whistling sound and smelled smoke. *What the hell is happening now?* I went into the barrel room where various smoke alarms were going off and the whole place was full of smoke. I went into the kitchen, and swear to God, I couldn't see any faces for all the smoke.

"Are you guys okay?" I wasn't sure they were guys since I couldn't see, but oh well. I asked why hadn't they turned on the fan.

"What fan?" they responded. I went over to the wall and turned on the fan. I then went and found Jim, who got on a ladder to turn off the alarms. We opened all the doors to air out the room and delayed the guests entering for another fifteen minutes so that we could get rid of some of the smoke. The guests were asking what was burning. We ask all new caterers and vendors to visit and familiarize themselves with new venues and know where the fire extinguishers are.

One very interesting wedding was at a private home, which was more like a private estate. The family's private chef was doing the catering. The guest count was about forty. Jim and I visited the home and it was amazing. The owners had strict rules for staff and guests. Shoes were to be removed and cleaned as guests entered the home, so I hired a young man to welcome the guests and wipe and store their shoes upon entering. The small ceremony was to be held in the dining room, and cocktail hour and dinner in the piazza off the living room, with no dancing. The bar would be set up in the library in a small alcove between incredible artwork and priceless statues.

I was asked to hire a caterer's assistant to help their private chef, so I asked one of my favorite caterers and was able to hire one of their very experienced chefs to assist. I ordered all the rentals chairs, tables, linens, china, flatware, and glassware. I hired live musicians to play for the ceremony, cocktail hour, and dinner since they did not expect dancing. I hired the serving staff and bartender. I ordered the cake and flowers, and we were set. The owners and parents of the bride were on a three-month cruise before the wedding, so we were able to oversee all the services.

As I mentioned, the homeowners were very specific as to the rules for their beautiful home. The rentals were delivered the day before the wedding, and Jim and I were there to oversee the set up. The homeowner insisted that the Chiavari wooden chairs have felt put on the tips of the legs as to not damage the hardwood floors. They offered their houseman to do this chore. The china and glassware was counted out and set up in the kitchen, and Jim and I folded the napkins and laid out the linens to be dropped on the table the next day.

The day of the wedding, the staff we had hired arrived with Jim and I. The chef's assistant was already in the kitchen assisting their personal chef. Our gals placed the linens on the table with the napkins and then the glassware. Our bartender set up her bar with wine, beer, and mixed drinks. She was told no one was to come behind the bar or get too close since she was set up between this very expensive artwork. She was also not to fill the drinks too full since the homeowners did not want any spills, and none would be tolerated.

Guests arrived, and our welcome gentleman and shoe cleaner invited the guests into the hallway, took their shoes, cleaned them, and placed them in a closet, marking which shoes belonged to whom. One of our staff was bearing a tray with Champagne while soft music was being played in the living room. A pianist and violinist provided the music. After a fifteen-minute welcome, the guests were invited into the dining room for the ceremony. The ceremony was provided by a rabbi who was also a friend of the homeowners.

A cocktail hour followed in the piazza and guests were welcome to go to the bar, which was in the art room adjacent to the piazza. Guests were enjoying tray passed appetizers and great drinks. After an hour of cocktails the guests were invited to be seated for dinner. The bride and groom wanted an informal entrance and walked in with their guests. There was a welcome toast by our homeowner and dinner was served. The food was amazing and wine was poured at the table by our staff. Dinner was relaxed with a few toasts thrown in informally by friends.

After dinner the two-tiered cake was cut and served, and the bar was open again for guests to enjoy and mingle. Our bartender was carefully pouring drinks and watching guests for mishaps. I checked on her on a regular basis while our other staff cleared the tables and rinsed and stacked the china and glassware for pick up the next day. I went back in to check on the bar and guests, and I noticed the house man with a toothbrush cleaning red wine off of the wall by the bar. I asked our bartender what had happened, and she said that a guest had leaned against the wall and had inadvertently spilt some wine on the wall. Our unhappy host ordered his houseman to clean up the spot with a toothbrush.

He also told me to close the bar, that we were done. Once the bar was closed, the guests did not choose to linger. Shoes were given back and guests departed. Jim and I and our staff finished racking glasses and china, bagged linens, and swept up the dining area. The chefs cleaned up the kitchen. I paid our staff and thanked them, and we were done and out of there. The following year, the same homeowner asked us to plan another party for him, and I declined, saying that we had another event for that day, but thank you. The stress of perfection, and the priceless artwork was too much for my nerves. We survived it once. Could we survive a second time?

We have also used food trucks at private estates, and even though the food can be very good, the wait time makes toasts and announcements difficult. While the last of the guests are outside waiting for their meal, the first half is already done and waiting for something to happen. You can't start the toasts or dancing unless everyone is in the same room at the same time. It not only throws off the timing, but then you need to hire a second crew for clearing, bussing, and cleanup. If you want a casual wedding and are not concerned with timing, then the food trucks make a good option.

My older and younger daughter went to a friend's wedding where the family had provided the food and the set up. Guests could help themselves to the wine and beer set up at a separate station from the food table. Dinner was a buffet where guests could help themselves, and the food was replenished by friends. The only issue was that the plates remained on the tables with bees and bugs drawn to the plates. Debbie, a professional bartender, and her sister found this unacceptable, and they started bussing tables. The bride's mom told her this was not necessary, but both girls said they couldn't stand to see the mess on the tables. I had trained them early and well.

A good point to remember if you choose to make it a do-it-yourself family wedding: please hire or assign people to replenish, clear, and clean up. It's not fair to the family members to have to do this at the end of the night when they're already exhausted from the set up and the evening. A wedding is a lot more work than you think.

Chapter 13:

Injuries and Mishaps

WHEN YOU'VE DONE AS MANY WEDDINGS as we have you are bound to have injuries and mishaps. Some were serious, and some not so serious. Weddings and alcohol don't always mix. One wedding the groom and his guys and been out playing golf before the wedding and it was a hot day. The guys were lined up to walk down the aisle. Guests and family were already seated. Music was cued and the guys starting walking. They had to walk down some stone steps. I normally give a hand wave for the music and then a wave to the guys to walk. Four of the guys started walking but the fifth wasn't coming. I hurried up the steps to check on him and he was down. He had fainted, hit his head, and was out like a light with a gash on his head. I motioned for the officiant to keep going while I called 911 on my cell and stayed with him until the paramedics arrived. I led the guests up another route to the cocktail hour so the party and guests would not see the poor guy. I told the groom, but no one else. At the end of the night, the groomsman arrived back at the winery, sober and with his head bandaged. He was going to be fine, but he missed the whole evening. He admitted that he had also consumed a lot of beer while golfing and he might have overdone it a bit.

Another exciting evening was at a resort wedding. The bridal party was fun and from England as was the groom. I mention this only because the guys told me, "Brits love to party," and yes, they do.

The ceremony and dinner went well. We got to the dancing party of the evening when things got very lively. Two of the groomsmen were dancing together, and one decided to do a backflip over the other groomsman. There was a large fireplace and hearth in the room designated for dancing. You guessed it, the one groomsman hit his head and there was blood everywhere. He was conscious and on his feet, but what a mess. I called 911 again, and the venue manager insisted that he be checked out. The groomsman refused to go in the ambulance. The bride's dad was a physician. He put on a few butterfly bandages, and we applied an icepack and he was back on the dance floor.

Jim again came to pick me up from the venue he was working down the street, and the ambulance was just leaving. Jim asked, "What did you do this time?"

I said, "Absolutely nothing. Brits just like to have fun."

It seems to always be the guys that get hurt or at least do stupid things. We have had brides faint at the altar and had to sit in chairs for the ceremony. We have groomsmen and the groom faint from the heat, but most times the injuries are from silly, or should I say, stupid behavior.

One very warm August night, we had done a wedding at a private winery in the Valley. Dining tables were set up around a small lake, or actually a large pond. Dancing would be in the barn. All was going well, though admittedly, it was uncomfortably warm. In the middle of dinner, one of the groomsmen stood up, stripped off his tux down to his skivvies, and jumped in the lake. Then, of course, the other guys followed suit.

The owner of the property came over to me and said, "Get them out! It's not sanitary. The cows drink from there. Get them out!" Sure, no problem, I'll just grab one of these slippery, slimy guys and haul them back to shore. Thank goodness, the groom interceded and convinced the guys to get out, get dressed, and show some decorum. Not sure why I get the weddings that people decide to strip. I did not hear if any of the guys got sick, just some bruises from hitting rocks in the pond. I cringe every time I hear the expression, "Go jump in a lake."

Another example: one groomsman, at the very end of the evening, was goofing around outside with other groomsmen and decided he could jump down a short flight of stairs. Apparently it was a dare. The bride and groom were saying goodbye to the last of their guests and most of the guests had already left, thank God. I heard a scream and then someone yelled, "Someone get ice!" I went outside to see what was happening, holding a bag of ice. Here was this poor guy lying at the bottom of the stairs with his femur, the largest leg bone, sticking through the skin. Great, a compound fracture. Again, 911 was called, and he was transported to the local hospital. The event manager and I proceeded to pour buckets of water on the steps to get out the bloodstains. We had another wedding there the next day plus winery visitors, and we didn't want them to see this bloody mess. My favorite DJ was working with me that night and his significant other is a surgical technician at the local hospital. She had just come out of surgery and was heading home when she got the call to come back for this gentleman. She was there all night while he went through surgery. The next day both the DJ and I heard about her ruined evening by our unruly guest. Could we please try to do better in the future?

It's not always the guests that get hurt or do stupid things. I fell down the steps one night at a wedding when my heel on my shoe broke, sending me down the stairs. Thank goodness it was close to the end of the night, nothing was broken, and ice and bandages were enough. My pants and shoes were ruined, but I would survive. I wasn't even drinking. Jim has hit his head, cut his arm, and strained his back from lifting. We carry Advil, Benadryl, bandages, and Ben Gay in our emergency kit. I try to keep up on my CPR skills and am very good with Ace bandages on ankles and elbows.

Two of these accidents happened to me on our busiest wedding weekends, Memorial Day and Labor Day. One Wednesday ten years ago, just before Memorial Day weekend, Jim and I were involved in a car accident. My youngest daughter and grandson were in town visiting and were also in the car. We were broadsided by a truck that ran a red light. Thank goodness no one was injured other than me. I had been turned sideways and hit my left side on the console. It turned out that I had bruised my spleen and it was bleeding. The doctors were able to stop the bleeding and kept me in the hospital until Friday morning. I had a rehearsal that afternoon and weddings on Saturday, Sunday, and Monday. The doctor told me I could do the weddings if I did not lift, bend, or turn. Great. I could do this, just load up on Advil. Just riding in the car with my seatbelt on hurt so bad that it was hard to take a deep breath. My four-year-old grandson loaned me a stuffed rabbit to place over my side under the seat belt. I carried this stuffed guy with me for three months. It took seven weeks to heal, but I had grown attached to the rabbit and he became my security rabbit. We survived the weddings: the caterers, Jim, DJ, and photographers would not let me do anything but talk and give orders. As long as I stood tall and didn't turn quickly, I was fine.

Six years later, on a very hot Labor Day weekend, we had four weddings; Friday, Saturday, Sunday, and Monday. The first wedding on a Friday night was outdoors at a resort up Valley. It was so hot, 112 degrees, that the family rented air conditioners for the outdoor lawn ceremony. The florist was afraid to put out the flowers since they would wilt the minute they were placed at the altar. The dinner and dancing was in a cave, which, thank goodness, made it bearable for the guests. We got through the evening fine, and when I got home, I noticed that my left foot was hurting, itchy and swollen with little bumps and blisters all over it. I soaked it and iced it, adding antibiotic ointment, and then went to bed. I assumed correctly that something had bit me.

Saturday's weather was hot again, but inside it was tolerable. Guests consumed more beer and chilled wine than usual, and everyone was in good spirits. When I got home my foot was even more swollen. Jim wanted to take me to the hospital, but I had two more weddings to go, so again, I soaked, iced, added ointment, and then drank more wine.

Sunday my foot looked so bad that I covered it in bandages so as not to frighten the guests. I wore sandals because I couldn't fit my foot into shoes. I was limping, but we made it through.

The Monday wedding passed the same way as Sunday; happy couple, happy guests, same old stuff. My own wine consumption also increased. By the time I got home at one in the morning, I sipped one or two glasses of Chardonnay while soaking my foot.

By Tuesday, I went to the doctor and my foot was infected from yes, spider bites. Thank God I hadn't seen the culprit, or I would have passed out and never made it through the weekend. I was put on antibiotics and told to elevate my foot. He chewed me out for not coming in sooner, but, dammit, I had a duty to my couples.

I'm not the only one that had to tough it out. One of my bride's mothers had her gall bladder out three days before the wedding. She was obviously in pain and couldn't dance; actually, she could barely stand, but she was there. What a trouper.

Another mother fell a few days before the wedding getting off the plane. She broke her ankle and was on crutches the entire evening. Her Jimmy Choos never got worn. I've had parents with terminal illnesses that made it for part of the evening or just for the ceremony, but at least they were there for the couple. One mother of the bride had been so ill with cancer that she could not eat the food that the caterer had prepared. One of her friends pulled me aside and told me the mother couldn't eat solids, and asked if I could get the food pureed. The caterer did not have the equipment to honor this request, so I asked Jim to go to one of our favorite restaurants right up the street and get a bowl of soup. Jim asked them to just give him broth. The restaurant was so kind. They mixed up a double batch of broth with pureed vegetables, and we served this to bride's mom. This was the only meal the mother could eat all evening. Some nights just break your heart.

Another wedding, we had a groom that had hurt his back and ruptured a disc about two weeks before the wedding. He was on pain pills and was in agony. Before the wedding, he couldn't even stand to get through the forty-five minute rehearsal. He would lie down on the ground every chance he got. His face was absolutely grey. I pulled his mother and the bride aside and asked, If he can't stand now, how will he make it through five or six hours tomorrow?"

His mom responded, "Well, he can't, I guess, but what option do they have?" We decided we needed a place for him to lie down whenever he needed to. This winery had no side rooms or private areas close to the dining area, so we decided to rent a chaise lounge, put it in a small alcove, and hang a sheet or something over the entrance for privacy. I had already placed the rental order with linens and décor, so I was able to add a chaise lounge.

We hung a black sheet at the entrance to the alcove, and we had a private area for him to relax. Our poor groom used this area off and on all night. He made it through the ceremony but could not make it through dinner. The bride sat at a table alone until joined by one of her bridesmaids so she wouldn't have to eat alone. The groom was served in his private area. The groom could not do the first dance nor dance with his mother. The photographer was limited in the shots he could get and made the most of the ones that he could. It was sad and unfortunate, but both the bride and groom put on the best face possible. I got a letter two weeks later. Our groom had back surgery and was feeling much better.

One couple got too exuberant in their dancing, and the guest spun his date into a pillar at the side of the dance floor. She hit her head and started screaming at this poor, befuddled guy. He picked her up and carried her into the bar and laid her on the counter. "Somebody do something!" he yelled. I was already in the bar area boxing up the gifts, so I got a bag of ice and put in on her head. I asked if she wanted to go to the hospital. Her head was not bleeding, but she was developing a large bump on her forehead. When she continued to shriek and swear at her date, we decided to call 911.

The paramedics happened to be down the street getting a hamburger, so they arrived within ten minutes. After checking her out, they decided other than some bruising, she would be fine. They told us to keep ice on her head, and if she felt worse she could go to a local hospital. At the end of the night when they and all the guests left, the injured young lady was still not speaking her date. He kept mumbling that he didn't understand why she was so mad, accidents happen, you know. We now have 911 on speed dial.

Most of these accidents or mishaps could have been avoided and were minor, but some of the sorrow and tragedies we witnessed were unavoidable and maybe part of a bigger picture that none of us are meant to understand. One sweet bride lost her mother two days before the wedding. We did continue with the wedding as her mom wished, but it was another heartbreaker.

I did a wedding four years ago at a hotel resort in the Valley. Everything and everyone was in place and ready to go. Three days before the wedding the bride called to tell me that the groom's father had suffered a bicycle accident and was in the hospital on life support. The couple was debating canceling the wedding, although some guests were already on their way from the East Coast and other areas. I expressed my sympathy and would let the vendors know the wedding might be canceled.

The next day the bride called again and said the wedding was on and the groom's mother thought that her husband, the groom's father, would agree if he could. I notified the vendors that the wedding was still on. We made it through a quick rehearsal; no one was in the mood for chatting, and the bridal party just wanted to get through it. The groom's mother stayed at the hospital and missed the rehearsal.

The day of the wedding everyone was somber but we were determined to make the best of it. I had brought my favorite assistant since Jim was performing a ceremony in another town. The bride was having hair and makeup done when we checked on her. She was literally putting on a good face, and she looked amazing. We checked on the ceremony site, cocktail hour, and outside dining site, and then the barrel room for dancing. It was a beautiful fall day and the bride and groom wanted dinner outside. This property is very large with sprawling lawns, fountains, hedges, and lots of flowers.

An hour before the wedding Jim called me on my cell phone to say it was starting to rain up Valley. Impossible! The sky is blue and no clouds, just some wind. The tables were set with linens, glassware, and flowers, and my assistant was just finishing putting down the place cards for assigned seating when we noticed just a few random rain drops. I wanted to wait a few minutes before checking in with the bride. The musicians were in place, and we could put them under an alcove if needed. I talked to the venue manager, and she felt and I agreed that we should move the dinner into the barrel room. We frequently have dining and dancing in the large barrel room. It's a beautiful room with brick walls, good lighting, and large enough for both dining and dancing.

More drops started to fall and I hesitantly approached the bride. She had wanted the ceremony and dinner outside. This meant so much to her, and she had already been through so much that we didn't want to distress her more, so we agreed to go with her original plans and hope for the best.

As soon as the ceremony started, it began to rain harder. The guests were getting soaked and were heading under the alcove with the musicians. My assistant came over and told me that the linens were getting soaked and she was pulling the place cards off the table so that they wouldn't be ruined. When the ceremony ended, I approached the bride and told her that dining would be just about impossible outside, and we should move it in the barrel room. She tearfully agreed, but kept asking, "Why me? First my father in law, and now the rain! Why? Why?" None of us could answer why, and we all shared in her tears.

We all agreed we would make this a beautiful wedding, if not unforgettable. We could save this day, even if we couldn't stop the rain or help the groom's dad. We sent the bride and groom back to their room with the bridal party to dry off and freshen up. We would need an extra hour to flip the dining from outside to inside. The musicians and the guests were moved into a side room for a quickly set up cocktail hour. This room held a small fireplace and couches and chairs and was often used for elopements or meetings. The guests enjoyed drinks and appetizers and towels were passed out.

The wet linens and napkins were taken to a laundry room on the premises and quickly put in dryers. Tables were moved from the lawn to the barrel room. My assistant found a blow dryer and was drying the wrinkled place cards and guest book. We adjusted the tables the best we could to match the diagram from outside. A bar was set up inside. The flowers were moved inside and placed on the tables the minute the dried linens were down. Everyone pitched in—the DJ was helping the florist, the florist was helping my assistant. We made the transition in one hour and fifteen minutes. Every vendor wanted this wedding to succeed and maybe get a little smile out of this wonderful couple.

When we were set up and the room transformed, we invited the guests to enter the barrel room and be seated for dinner. Wine was poured and the bridal party and then the bride and groom made their grand entrance into the barrel room. The DJ was ready for the bride and groom to share their first dance. Dinner was served, and it was perfect. This venue has a great catering staff and chef. Thank God. I wasn't up to dealing with anything else.

The rest of the evening went well. The toasts were kind but solemn; all of the guests were aware of the tragedy that is family were living through. The bar was not the busy, raucous center of attention that it normally is during a wedding. When the groom danced with his mother, there were no dry eyes. Right after this dance, the groom's mother left to return to the hospital. The evening continued with dancing. It was overall a very pleasant but quiet wedding. I received a call a few days later and was told the groom's father had been removed from life support and had passed on. What a heartbreaking time when it should have been so joyous. I think of this wonderfully brave couple often. They were amazing, strong, and dignified though the entire time. Not sure I could have been as brave.

Chapter 14:

Dresses and Clothing Mishaps

We have several dress and other clothing disasters the day of the wedding, where quick thinking and a needle and thread (or staples) are needed.

I remember one wedding I did about eight years ago at a small hotel in the Sonoma area of the wine country. I was the officiant and coordinator, and since this was a small wedding of under fifty, I should be able to handle both duties.

I arrived an hour before the wedding and did a mic check with the DJ. Twenty minutes or so before the wedding the bride arrived, and I checked in with her. We were getting ready to seat guests, and I wanted to make sure they had the license and ask who would have the rings. She was adjusting her veil when I noticed this huge black stain on the back of her dress. "Excuse me, but did you sit in something? You have a large black stain on your bottom," I asked the bride. Better to be blunt, right?

She said, " Oh my God, my eighty-five-year-old father wanted to drive me over, and I must have sat in something."

"Okay, don't panic. I've got this," I said. I went into the kitchen and got two white napkins, wet one of the napkins, and put Joy dishwashing soap on the wet napkin. I then started in on her dress. I was able to get out most of it. Scrub, blot, and repeat. When we were done it was barely noticeable, although she did have a wet butt for a bit. I learned this secret when we had the bridal store. You can even put a gown in the bathtub or washing machine on mild. No dryer, of course. After speaking to the bride's father, he told me that he had transported a carburetor in his car before he picked up the bride. He didn't even think about the grease.

I have used this scrub and wipe method many times over the years on gowns and veils. Any dishwashing soap will work, Joy, Dawn, just as long as it's a liquid detergent.

Another wedding at a winery, the bride was putting on her gown for photos when she said she couldn't breathe. The bride's mother unzipped her and told the photographer to find me. The dress was suddenly too tight and she couldn't take a breath. The photographer found me and Jim setting up in the barrel room. We were one hour away from the ceremony. Upstairs we went, and it seemed the dress was too tight once it was zipped. She had not gone to her last fitting, and the seamstress had taken the seams in too much. She was in tears, and Mom kept telling her to relax. "I'm sure you'll be fine, just relax." Right, Mom, while she turns blue.

Okay, what to do? I can't sew, so I was useless even though I carry a kit with needle, thread, and other necessities. Jim, however, can sew and helped our seamstresses in the store once in a while, especially with the tuxedos. He can hem, sew on a button, and do simple tasks. Jim told me to get the sewing kit while he checked out the zipper and seams.

To make this short, Jim pulled the dress lining together going around the inside of the zipper, giving our bride about a half-inch more breathing room. He sewed the linings together with small, tight stiches. You absolutely could not see this, and whoopee! She could breathe. She walked down the aisle right on time. The seams held all night even with the dancing, dipping, and spinning. Jim, what a guy!

We must have used Jim's sewing skills ten or more times over the years. One day the mother of the bride's zipper went out on her dress minutes before the ceremony. Jim sewed the zipper together, and no one was any the wiser. Why it always happens before the wedding, I don't know. Not sure what I'd do if Jim was not there. Maybe I should learn to sew? Nah.

Another day, it was the bride's father in his dress blues. He was a military man and his pants were very tight. When he bent over, yes, right before the wedding, the pants split up the back. Jim stitched him in, and he walked her down the aisle. We did remind him not to do any serious bending during dancing; however, he could sit. The pants also held all night.

I remember one wedding where one of the bridesmaids was the issue. She didn't have trouble with her dress; she just didn't want to get dressed. The bride was ready, and all the girls were dressed and ready except for this one bridesmaid. The bride told her several times she needed to get dressed, that we were getting close and the photographer was getting the last minute pre-wedding photos. The bridesmaid insisted that her husband had to be there to dress her and that her zipper often would stick. Personally, I think she wanted to steal some attention from the Bride.

Her two young daughters, also the flower girls, were in the room, and she told the girls to find their dad. I volunteered, as did several of the other girls, but no, her husband had to dress her. The bride told her we needed to hurry and to let somebody else dress her. "Fine," she said, and stripped, and I mean stripped. She had nothing on under her dress. No bra, no panties, nothing. She had an amazing body, some enhancements I would say, but who knows? I thought my photographer was going to faint. He turned red, turned his head, and said wow! The bride told her to stop showing off and put on the damn dress. She'd had enough of her antics. I think we'd all had enough. I was embarrassed for the little girls. To this day, the photographer and I laugh and say to each other, " Remember the naked bridesmaid?"

I always remind my brides that they can have sparkling or white wine before the wedding but no red, since I don't want the spills. We have had more than one disaster with red wine. One wedding, right after the ceremony and during the cocktail hour and photos, we had an accident with a guest and the bride. A nice woman came up to the bride to give her a hug and well wishes when she happened to spill red wine down the front of the bride's dress. The woman was horrified and the bride's mother went ballistic. She was screaming at the woman, "You ruined my daughter's wedding! Get out! Get out!" She then yelled at me, the caterer, and anyone that would listen, "Clean her up! I said clean her up!" The guest kept trying to apologize, but finally she and her husband left the winery. Jim and the caterer were blotting the dress, trying to get the stain out, and the photographer was trying to calm the mother. She told the photographer to shut the f—k up. By this time all the guests were watching this fiasco. The bride was crying and begging her mother to stop, that it would be all right.

"No," Mom said, "It won't be all right. Our night is ruined!" Aha, whose night was it anyway? Jim and the caterers were able to get most of the stain out using the same process—wet dress, dish soap, white napkin, blot, blot. The bride's mother never completely calmed down the rest of the night and was going to call the lady that had ruined her daughter's wedding and give her a piece of her mind.

Brides should also make sure that her dress is bustled before the dancing starts. Many dresses have been ruined and torn from being walked on, and by the end of the night the hem is in tatters. One of my brides came in during the reception and asked me to cut off the bottom of her dress, which was torn and dirty. We cut all the way around until the entire dress was floor length. She wanted to enjoy herself and not be hampered by the trailing train. The hell with the cost of the dress! It only gets worn once, right?

Also think about the style of your gown if you want to enjoy dancing later. Mermaid or very tight gowns don't allow for much freedom. Another bride who had a beautiful mermaid gown could not walk up the stairs after the ceremony. She had to take tiny, mincing steps to get down the stairs. After a few attempts to walk up the stairs following the ceremony, she just couldn't make it. The photographer trying to get his exit photos just yelled to the groom, "Pick her up!" and so the groom did pick her up and carried her up the stairs. It was a great photo moment, but sitting and moving was difficult for her the rest of the night.

The bride might want to bring a second, more comfortable dress to change into for dancing. One bride also had such a tight dress that she half sat, half stood for the meal, and then about an hour after dancing began asked Jim to go back to her hotel and get her a pair of sweats so she could finally enjoy her evening. Her hotel was located an hour away, and by the time Jim got back, the evening would be over.

Bridesmaid's dresses have become less about matching but more about comfort and letting the bridesmaid choose the style best for her body, often in the same color or fabric as the other bridesmaids. One very kind mother offered to make all the bridesmaids dresses (six) to save the girls money, and all the styles would be the same. The bridesmaids paid for the fabric, but the bride's mother would do all of the labor. The night of the rehearsal I asked why the bride's mother was not at the rehearsal and was told that she was home sewing to finish the bridesmaids' dresses. She had been up all night for several nights trying to finish the dresses. Well good luck, I hope she makes it.

The next day at the wedding when I met with the bride and her party to go over the line up again, and make sure everyone was ready, I was told that only one bridesmaid would be in the wedding since the other dresses had not been finished. The bride's mother would also not be attending since she was exhausted and overwrought by taking on this chore and not succeeding. It was sad for the bridesmaids that couldn't stand with their friend and for the groomsmen that didn't stand because it would look odd. It was very sad for the mother who didn't even come to her daughter's wedding, and most of all for the bride.

Please, moms and family members, don't take on or promise something that you may not be able to finish. Overall, the bride and groom's day was not as wonderful as it should have been.

We often will offer, for a small fee, to press the bride's gown or the bridesmaids' dresses. When the brides travel with their gowns or ship the gowns, they are usually wrinkled when they arrive. The bride can take them to the local cleaners for pressing, but that can get pricey. We have a professional gown steamer from when we owned the bridal store. We had kept one of two steamers since they are expensive to buy. Jim will normally do the steaming, since our steamer is heavy and the dresses normally take an hour or more to steam.

One bride had asked if we could steam her gown, and yes, Jim was glad to. He picked it up at the local hotel. Once he pulled it out of the bag, he was flabbergasted. The gown was a huge ball of tulle, seven layers to be exact. If the dress were helium, the bride would float away. We got the dress on Wednesday for a Saturday wedding. Jim started steaming, and it was so wrinkled he had to do one layer at a time: lay the dress out, then another layer, and another. You get the idea. It also had a very long twelve-foot tulle train. It was so big that he had to lay the dress on our bed between steaming. Since it took two days to steam this huge dress, we had to move into the guestroom to sleep. There was no room for the dress and us. Jim told me to remind him to never volunteer to steam a dress again. Of course, he is still doing the steaming, but he now asks, "How big is your dress?"

The morning of the wedding Jim delivered the beautifully pressed and steamed dress to the bride's hotel. He had the bride's mother help him carry it in since it was not in the bag but on a hanger so it would not wrinkle again. Jim had no sooner got back to our van when bride's mother came out screaming, " Jim, don't leave! The dress ripped!" When Mom had tried to hang the dress in the closet, she had inadvertently stepped on the train. The dress ripped at the waist. They had two hours to get the dress repaired and to the venue. Jim didn't feel he could comfortably repair this dress since it was so heavy, so he called me and asked what the name and phone number of one of the seamstresses that used to work in our store. Thank God Judy was available and told Jim to come right over with the dress.

The bride's mother insisted on going with Jim to make sure nothing else happened to this dress. Judy was able to repair the dress, and he and Mom met me and the rest of the bridal party at the venue. Another crisis averted. We now check out the dress before we volunteer to steam a wedding gown or bridesmaid dresses. We have also been hoodwinked into doing numerous dresses, tuxedos, and mother of the bride dresses. The bride will ship her gown to us and then say she has one or two simple little items for steaming, and we will find three bridesmaid dresses, groom and dad's suits, two mother of the bride dresses, and three white dress shirts. I have suggested we start taking in laundry for extra income. It would be easier than wedding gowns.

For several years when we had the shop we would get calls from the local hotels or resorts to pick up the bride's gown, steam it, and return it to the bride's room. Jim has become a very professional steamer and has done the very top of the line designers. Our steamer has become a lifesaver so many times. I also use it at the holidays for tablecloths, napkins, etc. It does a faster and better job than the average iron.

During wedding season it's very common to have three or four dresses hanging in our downstairs bathroom. Of course, the cat is locked out of this room, much to her annoyance. Once a gown is steamed it should stay out of the bag to prevent new wrinkles. Long veils are gorgeous but can be tedious when they get caught as the bride is walking down the aisle, either on the cement, bushes, or even the grass. By the end of the night, the veil is often full of holes and is ripped. We have seen the bride's veil be torn completely off her head as she walks down the aisle when it got caught on something. Frequently the veil is destroyed with holes before the ceremony ever starts.

During photos the long veils can be stepped on by the bride and others and be riddled with holes before she starts her walk down the aisle. The bridesmaids will whisper, "Don't tell the bride, she can't see it and she doesn't need to know." As soon as the ceremony ends and photos are done, we collect the veil to return to at the end of the night. I should mention Jim also steams veils, but it's tricky because they can be easily burned, so be careful if you try it yourself. Put a light dish towel over it so the veil is not exposed to the iron. Another secret: you can make a white veil or lace turn ivory by simply soaking them in tea. The longer the soak, the darker the ivory.

Fire, candles, and dresses and veils are not a good mix. One of our brides had candles on the stairs and down the aisle for her wedding. As she walked down the stairs, her tulle dress caught one of the pillar candles and caught fire. Jim was officiating, and when he saw this he ran up the aisle. I ran down the stairs, and Jim was able to beat the fire out with his hands and the wedding proceeded with little damage to the dress. A few scorch marks on the tulle, but it could have been much worse. I may start strapping a fire extinguisher to my belt.

This reminds me of the veil story. We had just gotten through the ceremony when the bride took off her very long veil and handed it to her mom to set aside. We had a table set up at the cocktail hour with photos of the couple and a memorial candle for passed family members. Oh, whoops! Mom casually threw the veil on the table, and poof, the veil was gone in seconds. All that was left was the melted comb. The bride's mother was devastated, but the bride was a good sport. "Hey, Mom, at least I wasn't wearing it!"

We always recommend candles on the dining tables for ambience and extra lighting during the meal. One night during dinner I thought I smelled something burning, kind of like burnt feathers. I started walking around the room until I saw this lady chatting with her tablemate and leaning over a candle. "Excuse me, but your hair seems to be burning," I said as I pulled the candle away and blew it out. She said she hadn't noticed. We patted her singed hair with a wet napkin and she went on chatting, no problem.

At another wedding, the florist had suggested pillar candles or lanterns with candles to give that extra lighting needed. The bride's mother said to save money, she would provide them herself. The day of the wedding she brought glass lanterns with a pillar candle inside with some greenery on top. However, the candles were really close to the top of the lantern. The florist placed them on the table along with the other flowers and it looked lovely. However, during dinner, I again started to smell something burning. I began looking for fire, and I heard guests calling out that their table was on fire. As I looked I notice more than one table on fire. I grabbed the first lantern, blew it out, and headed for the second table lantern, and so on. Most of these I could put out by blowing out the candle, but three of these lanterns had caught the flowers on fire, and I had to take these flaming lanterns outside and hit them with a hose. By that time, we had lost all the lanterns and the table light. The bride's teenage sister came up to me and said, "Well, that's what my mother gets. She's so cheap! I told her, but she didn't listen. I can't wait to tell her I told her so." Family love, it gets me every time.

We have occasions to have a fire pit for a s'more station. Some venues will allow fire pits and many won't. It is a fire hazard. One time the couple brought their own fire pit to the venue. It was wood burning, and they had also placed it under a wood awning. I went outside later in the evening to check on the supply of marshmallows and noticed something burning. I looked up and noticed the awning overhead was smoking and getting very warm. We immediately pulled the fire pit out into the open and gave the awning a quick hosing.

Now none of the venues will allow wood burning fire pits. Jim and I eventually invested in two propane fire pits that we can take to venues that will allow them. They are much safer and easy to maintain other than clean out the burned marshmallow ooze.

Chapter 15:

D.Js, Bands, Photographers, and More

EVERY WEDDING HAS EITHER LIVE MUSIC, a band, DJ, or even iPod music. Music can make or break your wedding or event. A wedding band is not always the same as a club band, and the same can be said of disc jockeys. I enjoy working with both, but you need to make sure that they are professional and understand the nuances of a wedding. We've had some wonderful bands and DJs. I obviously have my favorites. All vendors have to be on the same team and on the same page. I have a few examples of weddings that could have used a professional.

We had a band, ten years ago or so, that looked like they came off the streets of Berkeley after a rough day of classes. They were dressed in ripped jeans and were unprofessional as well as rude when they arrived for set up. But our couple had hired them, so we would make it work. We showed them the set up area, gave them the rules as to sound decibels, start and end times, and no alcohol for the vendors.

They would be provided dinner and could have sodas or water if they chose. I did speak to them two or three times about the loudest of the music per the venue rules and asked them to lower the volume. We discussed the times of the two breaks they would have either while guests were eating, toasting, or the cake cutting. We noticed after the first break that the music got louder and the guys seemed looser. Maybe this is their style. Jim suspected something else and checked outside where the guys had been smoking during their break. Jim found an ice chest full of beer and booze. Liquor is not allowed at any venue, and certainly not by vendors. Jim hid the ice chest in the closest dumpster. After their second break, the band came back into the room to continue the last half of the evening, and they were miffed to say the least. I approached them to remind them that the music is a hard stop at eleven o'clock and remind them of the last song the couple wanted to hear. I thought the leader was going to take my head off. At the end of the night as they packed up and were loading up their instruments, they asked us if we had found any items that they may have missed. We said no, were they missing something? They could not ask for the ice chest since they knew they were not allowed to have it, so it was not mentioned. When they left, they told us that they would never work at this venue again. Thank God. Oh, by the way, don't hurt yourself loading out.

We have also had bands that are family members. The bride's brother can play the guitar and the cousin is a violinist, and they would like to perform. I would suggest that you hire a professional band or DJ and then ask these family members to do a song or two, but not put the entire night on their shoulders. These relatives might want to sit and enjoy their dinner and dancing too.

I was surprised one time when I was told that a family member would be joining in for a song or two and would be accompanied by our DJ. I thought, *Here we go again.* However, this gentlemen had a fabulous voice, and it turned out that he was a famous vocalist from South America and very famous in his country. He did several encores and was great signing autographs for the guests.

One of our sweet grooms sang to his bride during the ceremony. He had a great voice, and the surprised bride was in tears. Actually, everyone was in tears. He was persuaded to sing a few songs later during the reception.

Another groom wanted his two teenage sons and a few of their friends to play a set or two during the dance portion of the evening. The boys had brought their guitars, drums, etc. However, neither bride nor groom had ever mentioned this to me or the DJ. My timeline had been reviewed and approved by the bride and groom several times before the wedding. When dancing was to start, I had the DJ announce that the dance floor was open. The groom came after me in a tirade, grabbed me by the arm, and hauled me outside. "My boys are supposed to play a few sets now, and their instruments are outside waiting to be set up."

I told him that would be fine, but I had not been told, so I would have the DJ announce the boys when they were ready. It would have been nice if he had mentioned this to me and the DJ in advance, but I was not going to argue with him. He was bigger than me. The boys set up and proceeded to play for the next thirty minutes. The guests did not dance since the so-called music was not something that you would call dance music, and I don't think the music was recognizable. This was the groom's attempt to show off his boys, and maybe this was an audition. I wasn't sure, but I stayed far away from the groom for the rest of the night. Please always let your coordinator, band, or DJ know if you plan to have surprise entertainment.

This last minute talent show has occurred more than a few times. A family member or friend will insist on performing with or without the bride or groom's permission. It's hard for the couple to say no, and unless they give me permission to pull the plug, the uninvited will perform. I have had to leave the room when the screeching became too much for my ears. I guess the entertainer thinks they sound better under the influence.

One pleasing experience was with one of our brides. She had a nice singing voice and had performed off Broadway several times. The groom was in the film industry but told me he was not a dancer and would not even do their first dance. So the bride decided to surprise him. When they entered the dining area after being announced, we had set up a chair in the middle of the dance floor for the groom to be seated. Our couple came in, and the DJ asked the groom to please be seated. He looked puzzled, but he sat down. The bride picked up the mic and proceeded to sing an old show tune, "I Don't Dance, Don't Make Me." It was a hit, and our big strong groom cried. These are the moments that keep us going.

Another issue that can happen with bands is that they need more space for their set up. Since we are often limited in space, I ask them to tighten up as much as they can so guests have room to dance and the caterers have space to get through with food service. Most bands are very aware of this and are willing to squeeze in, but a few will take more space the minute I turn my back.

I have had some great bands and am blessed to work with music brokers that understand the difficulty of working a wedding. The band has to work their breaks around dinner and toasting, make announcements when needed, and stop at a set time. I have learned to make sure they have sufficient water during the evening, food at least one hour before they perform, and have a green room for breaks. Most venues and wineries don't have a private or green room for these performers, but we make sure that we give them a somewhat private area with chairs and water.

I did a wedding some fifteen years ago where I had two bands, one jazz band and one East Indian band. I had the challenge of finding the space for two bands, a dance floor, and the dining tables all in one large winery barrel room. The Indian band would play as guests entered for dinner, and the guests were welcome to dance as soon as the bride and groom were announced in. The jazz band would play background music for dinner and then the two bands would alternate in thirty- minute shifts after dinner. This sounded fun to me, and both bands were given my timeline. I would cue them when it was their time to perform.

The bride and groom entered, stopped on the dance floor, and the Indian band started to play. Guests jumped up and joined the couple on the floor. After the first song, the guests were supposed to be seated for the first course of dinner service. After five minutes of music the catering manager is signaling dinner is ready to serve, let's go. I motioned to the band to stop playing. Nothing happened, and they continued to play for a full twenty minutes.

After the guests were finally seated, I went to the band leader and asked him why he ignored my signals and why they played more than one song. He responded, "It was one song. All Indian songs last at least twenty minutes." I then had to adjust the timeline to accommodate both bands. The evening was a success. At the end of the evening, I thanked both bands, and the leader of the Indian band showed me his hands, which were red and raw. This is what happens when you play for twenty solid minutes. I have great respect for these gentlemen.

I have had the privilege of working with Indian bands again, including belly dancers. The music is amazing, and the costumes and colors are fabulous. During the dancing, the dancers were throwing money, and the couples' mothers were picking it up off the floor and bagging it. It was killing me to see this money being ripped under the feet of the dancers: fives, tens, and twenty-dollar bills. "Hey, Moms, do you need help?"

I work with disc jockeys more than bands. Normally the DJs are more affordable and can provide the ceremony, cocktail hour, and dinner and dance music. I have a list of DJs that I love to work with. The same criteria go for DJs as bands. They should be wedding DJs and not club DJs. They should not self-promote but be there to play the music requested and make announcements. I don't like to work with a DJ that constantly chats on the mic while playing music. The evening is not about him or her. Most DJs can provide wireless lapel mics for the officiant, wireless handheld mics for toasts and announcements, up lighting, gobo lighting, and more. Some even provide photo booths.

Your DJ should be professional in dress and in manner. I have had some frustrating if not harrowing experiences with DJs that were less than professional. Some of these DJs were friends, or found online. Please check DJs out thoroughly as you would with other vendors. They should be prepared for last minute changes, loop the music if the bridal party is slow getting down the aisle, and be accommodating as to their set up. I have had inexperienced DJs play the wrong music, cut the music off in the middle of the procession, and one crazy DJ announced that the bride was coming down the aisle. What? Really? The guests couldn't see the bride or hear the music?

Often we will have live music for the ceremony and cocktail hour—a duo, trio, or even quartet for this two-hour period. We have some amazing musicians that we work with. Some can offer a vocalist or even bring a grand piano on site if chosen. This piano can be expensive, but wow, the sound of the music makes it worth it.

I have had more than one bad experience with DJs just as I have with other vendors. One of my grooms chose a DJ out of the Bay Area because he specialized in the cultural music that represented the bride and groom. The DJ did well during the ceremony and played the music on cue as requested. When it was time to announce the bridal party into the barrel room for dinner, I asked him if he had the list and names of the six bridesmaids and six groomsmen so he could announce them. He looked at me blankly and said, " I don't talk."

"What do you mean, you don't talk?"

"Well, I get nervous. I play music, but I don't talk."

No amount of begging could get him to talk. "Oh, Jim, come here, please?" I gave Jim the mic, the list of the couples, and the order that they would walk in. The only problem with this was that all the names of the bridal party were in a language that Jim could not pronounce. I told Jim, "Well, do the best you can. Try to mumble, and I'll clap really loud and maybe no one will notice." Jim did his best and mumbled his way through it. Of course, then Jim also had to make all of the announcements throughout the night: for the toasts, first dance, parent dances, etc. During the evening the groom came to me and asked why Jim was making the announcements. I explained about the DJ's fear of public speaking. He was incredulous. "What does he think he was hired to do? Tell him he's not getting a tip, and he better stay away from me tonight because I may deck him." Another fun night was had by all. Yes, make sure your DJ or band will make announcements. That should be part of their job description.

Another fun DJ was from out of state. Our bride was in the hospitality business in another state, and she had contacts for vendors and discounts. She actually trucked in her chairs, linens, glassware, and most décor. Her photographer and DJ were from her area. The day of the wedding came, and everything was set up. It was beautiful. I met the two photographers, went over the details, and they were very accommodating. The three DJs arrived with tons of equipment. They had lighting, a fog machine, sparkler machines, and enough power equipment for a small town July 4th event. I explained where the various power outlets were and went over the winery rules. They assured me there was no problem.

The florist had hung string lights around the barrels and pillars so the room was beautiful.

During the cocktail hour while the guests were outside the DJs started plugging in their many gadgets. Boom! All of sudden there was a loud noise, the smell of smoke, and then darkness. Jim called a winery manager and the VP of the winery came in just short of ten minutes. They had burnt out the circuit breaker and it couldn't be repaired that night. We lost all of the string lighting and they would have to divide their gadgets to other outlets around the room. I had the job of explaining to the bride that some of her lighting and some of her gadgets would not be working that night. The building is old, and the DJs should have asked some questions and permission before they plugged all of these gadgets in. They did do a nice job with the music, and the sparkler machine worked long enough for the first dance and the fog machine long enough to make the dance floor very slippery. I am not a fan of fog machines for that very reason.

Always make sure that your band or DJ is aware of any stairs at the venue or an elevator since they have a lot of heavy equipment to deliver and set up. One very distasteful DJ that the bride and groom had found in the Bay Area came to the venue and threw a literal fit when he saw the stairs. I showed him where to set up and explained that there was no lift or elevator. He would have to carry his equipment down the stairs. There are approximately twenty stairs to get to the barrel room where he would set up for dinner and dance music. He starting yelling that he had not been told that there were stairs, and he was not going to do it, period. I told him sorry, but you've been paid and you have the obligation, so get moving.

He then told me that he charges twenty dollars per stair and the bride and groom were going to have to pay extra. He said I should go tell the groom or he was leaving. I told him he could tell the groom himself since I was not going to ruin their day, and he could bill them later if he had to. He then insisted on seeing the groom himself. I led him to the groom. The groom and his guys were having photos done on the lawn in the back of the winery. I introduced the DJ to the groom since all communications had been by phone. The DJ explained his dilemma, ah, extortion plan, of twenty dollars a stair or hasta la vista. The groom could pay now or the DJ was leaving.

The groom was obviously upset but had no other option, so he took out all the cash he had, three hundred bucks, and gave it to the DJ. Then the groom told me to keep the bastard out of his sight for the rest of the night. The DJ got his money and did his job. He played the music but did little else. The caterers and photographers had heard about this from the groomsmen, and the DJ was shunned by all. Normally, the vendors are provided a meal, but the caterer decided that they were not going to feed the DJ, and they didn't. I communicated with the DJ only when necessary, and all went as well as could be expected with the definite chill in the air.

The groomsmen had told the caterers that the cash had been tip money for the vendors, so the vendors were as angry as the groom. At the end of the night as the vendors were loading out, the DJ asked the staff to help him carry out his equipment. Really! Good luck, buddy. The staff refused, and the DJ lugged it out piece by piece.

I got an email from the groom several weeks later. The groom and his buddies were police officers in the area where the DJ lived. I understand this DJ did receive an inordinate amount of parking tickets in the weeks following the wedding. What goes around comes around.

Another couple was having a small park wedding and the guitarist did not show up to play the ceremony music. I parked my car close, behind some bushes, and turned the car radio up. I tuned in to a classical music station so the bride would have some music to enter to.

Photographers and videographers are equally as important as your band or DJ. Your photographer should be familiar with the venue, and if he or she is not from the area, they should make an effort to visit the venue before the day of the wedding to know the rules of the venue, check out the lighting, as well as the best spots on the property to shoot. All venues have times that the bridal party and photographer are allowed to arrive and start filming.

In the early years of wedding coordinating some couples could not afford a professional photographer and I was able to work out a deal with our local college to hire photography students for a few hours for a set fee of one hundred to five hundred dollars depending on how many hours they worked. The students had good equipment if not great experience. The couple would let them know the shots they wanted with family, bridal party, etc. The student would do the best they could and then at the end of the day, the student would turn the rolls of film over to the couple. The couple could take the film to Kmart or Costco to have developed. These were the days of live film. Now most photographers use digital cameras. The students did a great job, and our couples were happy. It was a win for both the couples and the students, and the students were gaining experience.

I remember one wedding when my photographer did not show up at the church. He was a professional photographer that I had used in the past. My couple was from out of state and asked me to hire a photographer in their price range. The bride was a news reporter for a TV station in the Midwest and the photos were important to her.

The photographer I had chosen was doing a small elopement in the Bay Area in the morning and was to meet me at the St. Helena Church at three o'clock for a four o'clock ceremony. When he didn't arrive at three, I began to panic and tried phoning him several times with no answer. When it was obvious that he was not going to make the church ceremony, I asked one of the guests that had a professional looking camera around his neck if he could jump in and get the ceremony photos and maybe a few family photos after the ceremony. The gentleman actually worked with the bride and was a professional news photographer. I apologized to the bride and told her that the photographer was typically reliable. I couldn't understand what had happened.

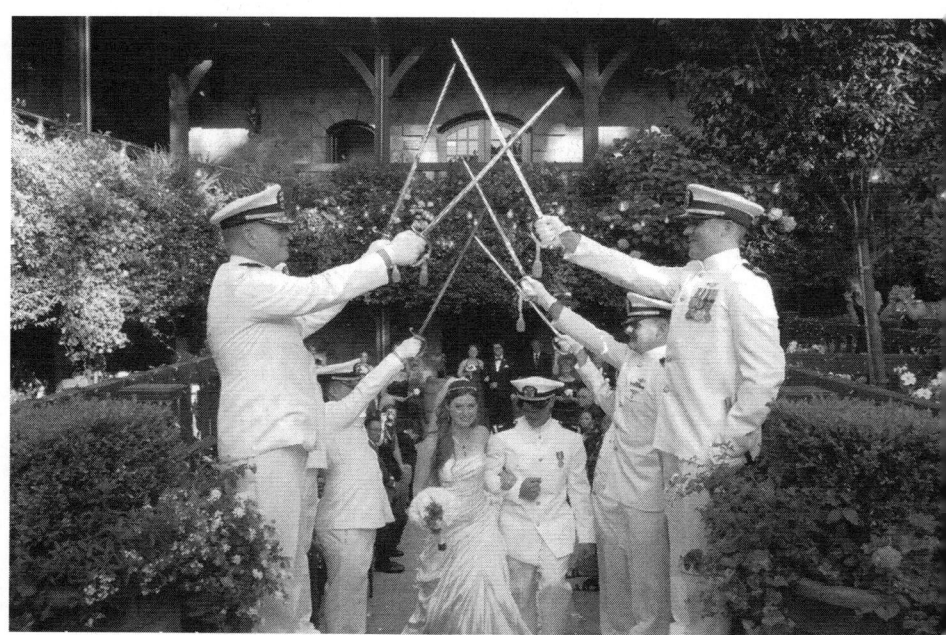

After the ceremony, the cocktail hour and dinner moved to a beautiful resort hotel overlooking the Valley. During the cocktail hour, my photographer showed up with a bandage on his head and a cast on his arm. "My goodness, what happened to you? I have been so worried, and I hate to keep asking this guest to continue to take photos."

My photographer explained that he had been involved in a car accident on his way back from the morning shoot. After being treated at the hospital for a broken arm and a bump on his head, he was ready to continue filming. He did finish getting all the family shots that he had missed and stayed until the end of the night to get the dancing shots, cake cutting, toasts, etc. He also gave the bride a refund for the time that he had missed. I could envision the bride on the news sharing the information that her Napa wedding coordinator let her down and her photographer a no show. I really should buy a good camera and learn how to use it, just in case. For my family photos, I use a throw away camera.

I did get into a standoff with one videographer and his two helpers. We were all set up for the early evening ceremony when the videographer was testing his lighting. He put a spotlight right on the altar into the eyes of the minister. The minister was doing a sound check and told me that he couldn't see to read with that strong light in his eyes. It was also obvious that this spotlight would ruin the ambience of the altar. I told the main videographer that he could not use the bright spotlight, at least not at the altar. He told me that if he could not use his spotlight, he wouldn't be responsible for the quality of the video films. I explained that other videographers have defused light and their work comes out just fine. "Well, I'm not other videographers and I am going to use this light, so get over it," he told me.

I responded that he was not going to use that light, and I would speak to the groom if he didn't back off. The minister also jumped in and expressed his thoughts. The videographer did back off, but only after he called me a bitch. "Yes," I said, "and proud of it." The caterers and I had to remind him throughout dinner service to tone down his lights. The bright lights can blind the caterers and the guests and ruin the atmosphere. Good videographers with good equipment don't need to use these blinding lights. If a videographer tries to convince a couple that he or she needs all that light, then you know that they are working with outdated equipment. Most of the videographers that I work with frequently use good equipment and are always respectful of the lighting and in preserving the ambiance of the venue.

I am proud to call many of these photographers and videographers friends. These people are professional, kind, and have the vendors back. These professionals have my respect for all they have to put up with and what they have seen. All too frequently, they are not respected but treated as the bride or groom's personal assistant.

Besides the stripper bridesmaid previously mentioned, the photographers have to put up with the family dramatics. They normally start working with the bride and her party at the hotel to get pre-wedding photos. They see the bride and her party with and without make-up and maybe not at their best. They often end up zipping dresses, finding water, and smoothing ruffled feathers. By the time they get to the venue they can already be exhausted.

I can get a read of the couple's moods from the photographer when he or she arrives at the venue. "She's easy and in a great mood," or "Watch out, she hated her make-up and made them redo it three times." They've sometimes said, "Her mother's in a mood, so get her a glass of wine quickly and keep her away from me for a while." That's when you know it's going to be another fun day.

Some photographers will just let the day flow and get some posed shots but more candid. Some photographers do more glamour and less candid. It depends on what the couple wants and the photographer's style. One photographer I worked with did beautiful work but was firm with her clients for posing and timing. "Let's not lose the light, stand over here, now pose," etc. One poor little grandmother pulled me aside and told me that the photographer was scaring her and asked me to make her stop. I spoke to the photographer. She calmed down and promised not to push so hard. These people are artists and see and think totally different than you and I might. But then, I can't even handle a Polaroid.

Some of the couples, more often the bride, are very demanding with the photographer. "Make sure you get my good side," "Don't get my butt," "I don't want my mother in law in the same photos with my mother," etc. Some of these brides can be scary in their demands. I often find myself calming the photographer as well as the bride.

One of our brides was so into the glam shots that she delayed the wedding thirty minutes while she posed with her girls on the lawn area while the guests were seated and waiting. When the groom mentioned that he had no pre-wedding photos with his groomsmen, the bride told him that the wedding was not about him and to stop sulking. The poor photographer was exhausted by the end of the night. We took bets on this one if the marriage would last a year.

One of my sweetest photographers came to me just before a wedding and told me that the bride scared the daylights out of him. She had caught her gown on her heel while doing photos in the vineyards, and then accused him of stepping on her gown. She said she was going to charge him for the cost of the gown. He was in tears and swore he hadn't been near the back of her gown. I told him to hang on, be professional, and don't engage with her other than doing his job. She was difficult to all vendors all night. When something like this happens, you just have to back off, be courteous and professional, and just do your job.

Another wedding, the groom demanded the photographer leave two hours before her scheduled time because at one point during the evening she forgot his name for a minute, and he said, "I hired you and if you can't remember my name, you're done." He came to me and told me to send her home. Later he tried to get out of paying her the balance, and it turned ugly between the two of them until finally a few months later a compromise was reached. I often feel like a referee or a mother. Oh, wait! I am a mother. Same thing, I guess – mom and referee.

Most of the time I work with great photographers and videographers that will bend over backward to get the shots the couple want, add in family shots that weren't on the list, and keep to a semblance of a timeline. The bride and groom should give a list of the photos that are important to them, a list of the family members that are to be in those photos, and make the family members aware so they stay close for photos.

I have had some photographers that are not professional and do not respect the timeline of the venue, caterer, or me. If after ceremony photos are scheduled for forty-five minutes to an hour, these photographers will take two hours, and then I have to find them bring them back in. Then the caterers are mad because their timing is off, the risotto is getting burnt, the salads going limp, etc. Again, everyone needs to be on the same page.

One particular photographer was not familiar with the venue and apparently had been hired on a recommendation from a friend. She was not a team player and did not want to cooperate with me or the venue on the timing. After the ceremony we like to get the guests to the cocktail hour and move the ceremony chairs inside for dining. So the ceremony site needs to be cleared rather quickly. We had suggested that she do family photos in advance at the ceremony site and then continue after ceremony photos in the vineyards or other areas of the winery.

However, this photographer would not budge, nor would she accept any advice as to other areas to shoot. The caterer and her staff came out to move the chairs inside for dining and to pick up the area. The photographer had lined up the entire family, thirty people or so, in the area needed to be cleaned. We asked her nicely if she could at least move to another side so that we could grab the chairs. The caterers had a lot to do in a very short time. The photographer was standing her ground and would not give an inch. She told us that she would be done when she was done, and if dinner was delayed, so be it. The bride and groom looked at her and then at me and the caterer. It was a standoff.

"Fine," I told her, "but if dinner is delayed and the dance time is reduced, it's on your shoulders." Hearing that, the groom suggested that they move to another area and try to stay on the timeline. The photographer was difficult to work with the rest of the night. It's important that all your vendors are on the same page as well as the same team. Unfortunately, I have seen too many photographers or other vendors that think it's all about them.

I recommend "First Look" photos, where the bride and room see each other for photos before the ceremony. Then they can have photos with the bridal party and immediate family, and then they only need a few photos after the ceremony and the bride and groom can enjoy the cocktail hour. The photographer will be around for dinner and dancing photos and can leave by ten in the evening or so. Don't pay for more time than is needed by your photographer or videographer. Also give your photographer some creative freedom to get those wonderful spontaneous or sunset photos beside the set family photos that you want.

These vendors are the unsung heroes and don't get the credit they deserve. I have had a photographer fall of a ladder shooting a wedding. Her leg was bleeding and she wouldn't stop long enough to let me bandage her leg. She later needed stitches. I have watched photographers and videographers get berated for trying to keep on schedule, or for them taking a bathroom or quick meal break. I've had brides yell at me, "Where is that damn photographer? I want this photo with my sorority sisters."

"I'm sorry. He took a three-minute bathroom break."

One bride got upset when the photographer was not there for her bouquet toss at half past ten at night. The photographer was scheduled out at ten o'clock. I had put the bouquet toss in my timeline for after the cake cutting, well before ten o'clock. But during the reception, when I reminded her and handed her the bouquet, she told me that she was having fun and we could do it later. When I finally I cornered her to toss the bouquet before the guests left, she asked where the photographer went. I explained that the photographer had left. She had been reminded of the toss before they left. She then spat at me, "How dare those bitches leave? They knew this was important to me!"

Right, those terrible bitches that had been with the bride since eight o'clock that morning; how dare they want to go home and get off their feet? Thank goodness this is not the norm and most couples are kind and grateful to their professionals. I have seen four thousand dollar cameras dropped and broken during the evening. The cameras are heavy and most photographers suffer from back issues. I work with three photographers that always work overtime with no extra pay. I will tell them, "Go home. You're done," and they'll say, "No, it's okay. I just want to get a few more minutes of the dancing," or take the couple outside for a night photo. No charge, it's all about their work and their vision. These people are true artists with big hearts. Love you guys. You know who you are.

Chapter 16:

Attire, Appropriate and Not So Appropriate

WHO'S TO SAY WHAT IS APPROPRIATE TO WEAR to a wedding as a guest or family member? I have seen jeans and cut offs when the wedding invitation states black tie, and I've seen formal when the invitation states casual. Sometimes we literally see too much, if you get my drift.

Years ago we had a wedding for witches where the bride and her girls wore all black. The guys were similarly attired. The cake was chocolate cake with black frosting, with a cake topper of skeletons in the form of the bride and groom. The ceremony was non-traditional with lots of chanting. It was actually very fun, a little spooky but very informative, and no, the couple did not leave in a hearse or by broomstick.

We had one bride that loved the theatre, musicals, and Paris, so she came dressed as a can-can dancer, in hot pink and black with lots of ruffles and a slit up the side. She was as fun as her dress with lots of high kicks throughout the dancing. The bride and the bridesmaids actually did the can-can during the reception.

One of my brides was very well endowed. I believe *buxom* is the word. She had chosen a strapless dress. Well, the girls were busting out all night until they finally busted free on the dance floor. She was gently reminded by the groom that all was hanging out, but she just laughed and said, "Well, if you got it, show it!" In her case, "fling it!"

Thinking back, it's not just the brides that have challenging attire. It is also their mothers. Maybe they want to compete with the bride and just not admit that they're getting older. But I have had some come-to-Jesus conversations with the mothers at the bride's request. One of our bride's mothers came to the wedding in a skin-tight, leopard skin dress. She looked more like a hooker than the mother of the bride. Our sweet bride was so embarrassed and had begged her mother to behave, but it was all about mom. All night she flirted and slithered, much to everyone's amazement and to the bride's chagrin.

Another bride called me in tears that her mother was going to wear a white dress to her wedding. She asked if I would please give her mother a call. So I called her mother and explained the etiquette of not wearing white to her daughter's wedding, or anyone else's wedding for that matter.

"But I love this dress and it looks great on me," she said.

I suggested she wear it to the shower or rehearsal dinner but not the wedding. She continued to plead her case until I finally said, "NO. It's your daughter's day, so NO."

At a summer wedding a few years back, I did not have as much luck. The groom's mother picked out a dress in ivory lace that could have been a duplicate of the bride's dress. The bride called to explain the problem and asked my opinion. I told her to have her future mother in law select another dress. The bride's mother had picked out a lovely dress in shades to compliment the wedding, and the groom's mom should follow suit. The groom spoke to his mother, and she refused. She mentioned that the bride was being selfish and was trying to turn her son against her. I continued to chat with the bride about this and hopefully the groom's mother would see reason. The day of the wedding came. Not only did the groom's mother show up in the ivory lace dress, but she also refused to speak to me and gave me dirty looks every time she saw me. Sometimes, you just can't win.

Note on proper etiquette: the bride's mother should pick out her dress first, color and length, and the groom's mother should follow in shades chosen by the bride and the hem length the same as the bride's mother. It's not a contest of who is the hottest, but a matter of respect for the bride and groom. Both moms can be beautiful but also tasteful.

The groom, groomsmen, and dads have it easier—a nice suit or tuxedo will do. The guys have spruced it up with fun socks, tennis shoes, flip flops, or even hats. If the groom or groomsmen are in the military, they can wear their uniform. There is nothing more attractive than a man in uniform. If they are wearing a uniform, no boutonniere is necessary, and it's actually against military rules to pin a boutonniere on a uniform.

We also have done weddings where the guys are in Scottish kilts. It's not necessary to have great legs for this, just longer socks and hopefully underwear. I did one wedding where the entire bride's family was from Scotland and all were wearing the kilts in colors of their clan. My only difficulty that day was finding the bride's dad. His twin brother, his cousins, and most of his family resembled him and were wearing the same color kilts. It was difficult keeping track of Dad that night with all those matching clansmen.

Chapter 17:

Fights and Disputes

OVER THE YEARS WE HAVE HAD A FEW FIGHTS, both physical and verbal. Sometimes it was with guests, sometimes the bridal party. Here are a few examples of what we have seen.

One evening reception turned into a brawl on the lawn at the winery with ten to fifteen guys punching it out during the dance portion of the evening. The bridal party and guests were a mix of Marines and police officers. A dispute broke out over something said, and the guys decided to take it outside. The security guard on duty came to Jim and I when he couldn't break it up. The security guard was a little man of approximately seventy-five, so no, he couldn't handle it by himself. Jim and I ran out to the lawn area where pushing, punching, and shoving was going on. A few bodies were hitting the ground. I am yelling, "Stop or I will call the sheriff!" while Jim is trying to pull these much younger and much stronger guys apart. I told the guard to call 911 and proceeded to scold them like they were naughty children. "You should be ashamed. You're in uniform and not being very respectful of that uniform!"

One of the guys, after pushing another buddy to the ground, yelled, "Go ahead call the police! Remember, we ARE the police!"

Good point, he had me there. One of the guy's mothers pulled me aside and told me off. "How dare you call them disgraceful! Boys will be boys."

They finally pooped out and went back inside for more wine and beer. They were buddies again and all was forgiven.

Another evening, a couple that had attended the wedding together, I assume they were a couple, started fighting because he was flirting with some lady at his table. They were asked to take the fight outside but instead went into the tasting room where they continued to scream at each other. I asked them to please behave and not ruin their friend's wedding. At this point the young woman slapped the man, and he grabbed her and shook her. With the help of one of the catering staff, we were able to separate them, and the young man stormed out and left his date in tears and without a ride home. I wonder if they are still together.

Only one time did we have wedding crashers: four young women showed up at the winery where the reception was winding down close to eleven o'clock. The young ladies had been at a restaurant bar down the street, saw the lights, heard the music, and thought they would drop by. When they entered the room, I did not recognize them as guests, so I asked them if they were not guests to please leave. This was a private event. The bride and groom were saying goodbye to their guests and the music was winding down. One woman, I assumed the leader of the pack, refused to leave. I asked more firmly for them to please leave. The pack leader then told me I was being a rude bitch and how dare I ask them to leave. My favorite DJ, upon hearing this loud exchange, came to my rescue. He asked them nicely to leave and not make a scene. The bride and groom and remaining guests were watching this exchange from a distance. Pack leader told the DJ that I was a rude woman and spoiling their fun. The DJ was finally able to convince the four to leave, and he escorted them out to the parking lot. The DJ still teases me to contain myself and not be rude to the guests.

One Saturday evening, ten years ago or so, a guest who had too much to drink was harassing the staff and other guests, singing at the table and then making very rude remarks about female staffers and guests. When approached by a staff member and myself, he took a swing at the server and told him to "buzz off." We told the groom that we were escorting his guest outside and would ask him to remain in his car until the end of the reception. His keys were taken away and a friend said he would drive him back to the hotel later. It was that or a call to the sheriff.

At the end of the night when the guests were gone and we had finished clean up, I went out to my car to drive home. I had two flat tires. On closer inspection, they weren't flat. They'd been cut with a knife or some other sharp object. Had our nasty guest slashed my tires? How had he known it was my car unless one of the staff told him? I called AAA and waited fifty minutes for a truck to come and give me spares. After that night, I parked my car under good lighting and asked the security guard to do a parking lot check occasionally.

It's not always the guests that can be rude or difficult, but sometimes it's the family of the bride and groom. You would think weddings would bring out the best in families, but often we see the worst of these families. Families of the bride and groom don't always get along or even like each other. One wedding, it was between the mother of the bride and the mother of the groom. Both mothers were to be involved in the ceremony and to approach the altar to pour wine for the wine ceremony. Then they would return to their seats. I normally ask the mothers to turn and hug each other before being seated again. This shows solidarity between the two families, and it's sweet and good for photos. However, this one time the groom's mother refused to hug the bride's mother. She said, "I'm not a hugger, and I don't feel like it. I won't do it." Okay, well fine. The bride's mother was hurt, and this rift continued through the rehearsal and the wedding day. My goodness, what's a little hug between in laws?

Another time it was the fathers of the bride and groom. Both were from different cultures and countries. They seemed cordial enough at the rehearsal, but the night of the wedding, both sets of parents were invited to participate in a tea ceremony that we had set up on the dance floor. This would be done while guests were seated and just after the bride and groom were announced into the dining area.

Everything was set up for the participation between the two families and the bride and groom. When it was time to proceed with this ceremony, the groom's father refused. Both mothers and the bride and groom were already at this little table and waiting for the fathers. Since the groom's father didn't speak English, I just motioned with my hands to go out to the table. Then the bride's father approached, and they started to argue and push each other. I tried breaking it up, but I don't speak the language and they couldn't understand me. All I could do was pat them on the shoulders and gesture. Finally the bride's brother got between the two men and got the bride's father to participate in the tea ceremony. The groom's father never did and returned to his seat. The evening continued without incident, but it was very chilly between the families for the rest of the evening.

It's not uncommon to have divorced parents and step-parents involved in the wedding. Some of these divorced parents get along fine and some… not so much. We have had to separate them for seating for the ceremony and for dining. I wonder if they realize how much this hurts their children. It's such a special day. I wish I could tell them to just get over it.

One of these divorced mothers was so sweet, and I became very fond of her during the months we worked together planning the wedding. She told me that her ex, the bride's dad, had remarried to a much younger woman, a trophy wife. She said she had no date and didn't want to look pathetic. The parents walk out together after the bridal party and this mother said that she felt pathetic walking out alone. We laughed about hiring an escort. Jim was the officiant for the night, and at the end of the ceremony as the parents recessed, I asked Jim to walk over to the bride's mom, hold out his arm, and escort her out. It was a nice touch, and we laughed about it later that we would share joint custody of Jim.

At another wedding, the groom's parents did not approve of the bride and made it known. They came to the rehearsal and to the wedding but left immediately after the ceremony. They were very polite to me and the other vendors, but when I asked them to stay for dinner, they refused. They felt their son was marrying beneath his station in life. After meeting her parents and the bride, I certainly didn't see it.

The bride's father had actually loaned the groom money to finish his college education, so what was with these parents? I hate to use the word SNOB, but whatever it was, it hurt their son. What would the future be like when this couple had children? Would they refuse to see their grand-children? I have a very hard time holding my tongue on days like this.

At times I have to be a hard ass, and I don't enjoy it. Asking guests to leave during the ceremony is never fun. A very nice young man flew all the way from Nebraska to attend his best friend's wedding. The groom had invited his friend although an invitation had never been sent. Fifteen minutes or so before the procession when the bride was scheduled to walk down the aisle, the bride, looking down from a balcony where she was fin-ishing photos, spotted this uninvited young man. "What the hell is he doing here? Get him out right now! Get rid of him!"

Okay, not sure what this was about, but I went to the groom and asked if this man should or should not be here. Should I throw him out? The poor groom told me that the bride had never liked his buddy, and I should prob-ably ask him to leave although he had sort of invited him and he had flown all the way from Nebraska. Okay, I will nicely ask him to leave. I ap-proached the poor man and explained the situation. I said, "I'm so sorry, but I will have to ask you to leave."

When I spoke with him, he was so sweet, and yes, he would leave. He asked if he could watch the ceremony from behind a tree before he left. I told him that was fine, our little secret. I went back to the groom and told him that his friend would leave right after the ceremony. The groom's mom joined us and asked what the problem was. The groom explained and his mother was upset. She liked the young man and thought the bride was being a ridiculous bitch. She told me to let the poor guy stay. Okay, now, I'm in the middle again. I will tell the Bride that he was leaving and maybe she'll calm down and not ruin her own wedding. When I ap-proached the bride, her mother was with her. When I explained the situ-ation, the bride's mother said, "Oh for goodness sake, let him stay! You need to get over this. You can't control his whole life and tell him who can be his friends."

The bride relented and I told the young man he could stay. He said he didn't need to eat, and he would stay out of her sight. I assured him he would eat, and I would arrange a table for him with the caterer, far away from the bride. Sometimes I just don't get the pettiness, but it is the bride's day.

At the end of the night, I always put the gifts, money envelopes, décor items, and leftover wine (if the couple has purchased it) in one secure area for the bride or groom's family or friends to take at the end of the night. Sometimes there are five or six boxes of items that the couple has supplied for décor as well as gifts and wine, so all items are kept under close scrutiny until it's removed by the family.

This particular night there were five cases of mixed wine varieties left to take home. The caterers and winery personnel had stacked it on the bar and ready for load out. I always ask who is responsible for these items so I give them to the right person. This evening it was the bride's dad that was taking everything in his car. Just after eleven o'clock, when the music ended, a man came into the tasting room and asked for another glass of wine. He was told the bar was closed and the evening was over. He then proceeded to pick up a case of cabernet and walk out the door. I said, "Excuse me, but are you in charge of taking this wine? I was told it was the bride's dad."

He said he was helping the dad and carrying it to the dad's car. Just to be sure, I went out, found bride's dad, and told him about his helper. Dad said, "No, he's not helping. Stop him." I ran back into the tasting room where I was told this man had just taken a second case of wine and was heading toward the parking lot. I yelled at Jim and started running toward the parking lot. Jim was following me, with one of the catering staff and the bride's dad following Jim. We picked up the security guard, yep, the old guy, while we were running toward the parking lot. I'm yelling, "Put the wine down, we've called the sheriff!"

The man handed the second case of wine to his buddy to put in their car while he yelled back, "The groom gave it to me and I paid him for it!"

Yeah, right. We finally stopped him at the car and retrieved the wine. The bride's father was furious with the guest, and the guest and his buddy got in their car and left. How can a friend steal from his friends? I just don't get it.

Other thefts have occurred over the years. One night a guest walked up to the bar where one of the catering staff was pouring wine, and as soon as the server turned his back to the man, he grabbed a bottle and headed for his table. One of the staff saw it and alerted me. I followed the man to his table and asked him for the wine he had just taken. "What wine? I don't have any wine."

I reached down, pulled up the table linen, and said, "That wine," and I took the bottle. Then he told me he had paid for it and was willing to argue the point until his wife said, "Lay off and let her take the wine." Most venues will not allow wine bottles on the dining tables. For one you can't monitor the consumption and keep the guests safe. It's also a waste of wine having so many open bottles and then possibly not consumed.

I am always shocked at the gall of some of these guests. At the end of one evening, we had the left over wine boxed and stacked for the bride's family to take. A young woman came in and asked for another glass of wine after the bar was closed down. When the winery manager told her no, she continued to argue. As soon as the manager walked away, the young woman and her two companions came back. She grabbed a large Imperial bottle of wine that was on display, put it under her coat, and walked out laughing. I followed her out to the parking lot and told her to give me the wine. She laughed, handed me the wine, and said, "Well, you can't blame me for trying." Really? Was this just a one night theft and her first offense?

Groomsmen are always sneaking in booze or beer, which is not allowed by most venues. Wineries can lose their license by having hard alcohol on property. So we all try to keep a close eye on this. The guys will sneak in flasks, hide the bottles in their jackets, or even hide bottles under the dining tables. At the end of the night, we have found empty booze and beer bottles under the tables and in the bathroom. If we catch the guys with it, we'll take it away, and they can retrieve it at the end of the night when they're leaving.

Before marijuana was legalized, it was also a sneak-in item. Smoking is normally restricted to one area since the smoke is not good for the wine. It may get into the casks. We have to repeatedly ask guests to not smoke inside. On more than one occasion the winery staff, Jim, or I have gone outside and the smell of pot is strong. "Okay, Darlene, walk fast and tell them to put out the smokes," and go back inside. Most guests were good and would dispose of the evidence, but a few had to be repeatedly reminded.

One groom actually handed me a bottle of good whiskey and told me to hang on to this all night. It was important for the bottle to be in the middle of the action so to speak. I told him that hard alcohol was not allowed on the premises and I would hold it for him until the end of the night. He said, "No, you don't understand. My brother Scott is in the bottle."

Sure enough, his brother had died several years ago in his early twenties in a car accident. Because Scott enjoyed a life of partying, after being cremated, Scott had been placed in a whiskey bottle. Scott stayed with me all night held tightly in my hands. I had to repeatedly explain to the winery personnel, catering staff, and other interested parties that this was Scott the groom's brother. I hope Scott enjoyed his night; I tried to give him the best view of all the activities.

I've done a wedding where the ring was lost. The best man and groom's brother was responsible for the bride's wedding band and had it in his jacket pocket. Twenty minutes before the ceremony was due to begin the best man came to the groom in a panic. He couldn't find the bride's ring. It had been in his pocket a few minutes ago, and then he went to the bathroom upstairs and now it was gone. Okay, the hunt was on. I told the florist, photographer, and some of the catering crew. We would look around but would not let the bride know – she would panic. We checked the bathroom, the halls, and the bushes. Unfortunately this venue has wooden planks on a second level above the ceremony site. These wood planks have spaces between them large enough for a ring to fall through.

Under the planks are flowers and ferns. If the ring fell in there, we might never find it. Okay, don't panic, we'll make up a story about why the bride won't get her ring at the ceremony. The groom came up with a doozy, and a very good story, I might add. He said he would tell the bride, and everyone would back up this story, that the ring got caught in the best man's tuxedo lining and they couldn't get to it until after the ceremony when it would have to be cut out of the lining. Okay, that sounds good and plausible. When I went back up to line up the bridesmaids and the bride, the bride told me that was a crazy story and asked if this ever happened to other couples. I said, "Yes, occasionally. I've seen stranger things."

The ceremony went fine. The groom used her engagement ring for the ring ceremony. Later during the night, the bride mentioned it again, but the groom and the bridal party quickly distracted her. The last I heard, the ring had never been found. I would not want to be around the bride when the groom told her the real story. The best man offered to pay for a new ring.

I think some of our guests may come to the wedding already a bit under the weather or have been hitting the wineries. One of these ladies got a wee bit upset with me one night. The catering and winery staff keeps a close eye on guest wine and beer consumption. If the staff feels that the guest has had enough or is not handling it well, they let us know and we find a tactful way to cut the guest off. This evening, the lady was showing signs of intoxication, and one of the staff told the rest of us. We agreed to cut her off. To keep her from getting angry and making a scene, they told her that Darlene might let her have another glass of wine in thirty minutes. We just wanted to make sure that she was functioning on her own steam. Ten minutes would go by and we'd hear her calling, " Darlene, Darlene, where are you?" After confronting her several times to let her know that time was not yet up, I began to hide from her. I know, I was being a coward. When I heard my name, I would duck behind the bar until she ventured off looking for me outside. If she looked behind the bar, I would go outside. Thank goodness this was during dancing, so I was not as busy. The caterer manning the bar pulled me aside and told me that every time our wandering lady came to the bar and leaned over, her bosoms would fall out of her strapless dress. She was getting all kinds of attention. Okay, I have to deal with this; why do I get all the boob jobs? I let her find me the next time, and I pulled up her top and gave her a very small pour of wine.

I was also concerned on how she was going to get home; she couldn't drive. I tracked down her date, husband, whatever, and he was just as gone as she was. I found a friend of the couple who promised me that he would get them both back to their hotel at the end of the evening. I may not always be loved, but I am often wanted.

We had a lovely bride that was a professional ballerina and was in fear of a previous boyfriend/stalker that had threatened her if she was ever to date again, let alone get married. Her wedding was to take place at a resort hotel in the Valley. Due to this fear, private security was hired for the night. Every vendor was given a picture of this stalker and we were all on high alert. The bride was nervous and jittery all night, as was the poor groom. The boyfriend/stalker had threatened to kill the bride and her husband if she ever dared marry. All guests had been sworn to secrecy and nothing had been put out online, so we were as secure as we could be. The ceremony and reception went off well with no issues. Unfortunately it was not the happy occasion it should have been, with the bride, groom, and most of the vendors on high alert. I often wonder if she ever heard from him again. We have had security before for celebrities or politicians, but never to prevent a direct threat. Maybe I should start packing a rod.

Chapter 18:

Toasts, Blips, and Bloopers

TOASTS CAN ADD A FUN AND NOSTALGIC MOMENT to this special day. We always recommend that the bride and groom give us a list of those making toasts. If a guest asks us if they can make a toast, we will check with the bride and groom before allowing this guest to toast. Besides toasts taking up extra time, they can also be embarrassing to the bride and groom, and even to the other guests. We have had some doozies.

One particular wedding it was the groom's mother, who proceeded to tell the groom how proud she was for overcoming his addiction to alcohol, and how in his youth he had numerous drunken incidents and a DUI and had finally gotten help. This was very sweet and the groom should be proud of handling his addiction; however, the bride, her family, and the most of the guests were unaware of the groom's troubles. The bride was horrified and bride and groom immediately walked outside to have a private conversation. I think Mom may have been tipsy.

Often the worst toasts come from the groomsmen and friends of the groom. The DJ and I are often speechless or shocked by what comes out of these guys' mouths. One gentleman, I say loosely, proceeded to talk about the wild parties that he and the groom had gone to while in college. He talked at great length about the groom drinking too much, throwing up, passing out, and the groom's dog cleaning up the barf. When the groom woke up, he saw the mess, barfed again, and then lay down with the dog. The guests were trying to enjoy their meal, but many plates went back to the kitchen untouched.

One maid of honor giving her toast looked at the bride and said, "You understand that statistically your groom is the one to most likely murder you, so just keep that in mind." The bride looked startled, and the guests just laughed. I guess it is statistically true, that the victim normally knows their murderer. Did the MOH know something that the bride didn't?

Another toast given by the groom's grandfather told the couple that he hoped their marriage would last as long as his sixty-five year marriage did. "Yes, our sixty-five years went by like it was fifteen minutes. Well, if you were under water." Not sure if that was an encouragement from a happily married man. I think it's always wise to think before you speak.

We have literally taken the mic away from these reckless toasters. The DJ also can turn off the sound to the mic and then you have the toaster moving his mouth but no sound coming out. Often we are warned by the bride and groom that, no matter what, we don't let this or that person toast.

More than once it has been the bride's mother that has been denied the honor. One of our brides warned us that her mother was not to say a word and absolutely do not let her have the mic. Her mother was one of those "it's all about me" moms. We kept the mother away from the bride before the wedding and distracted her with questions about seating, décor, etc.; this had all been decided before, but I promised the bride I would keep her mother away. The welcome toast before dinner service is normally done by the bride's dad or the bride and groom. This is a simple thank you to the guests for coming, etc. This wedding, the bride's father was giving the welcome toast. The DJ would retrieve the mic from Dad, and then the other toasts would happen between the first and second course. Our DJ was on his toes and was ready to grab the mic from bride's dad and hurry back to his station. Bride's mom tried to get the mic from her husband and then the DJ, but our DJ was too fast and she missed. When it was time for the best man and maid of honor toasts, these two were cued as to give the mic right back to the DJ. No passing of the mic. The MOH and BM toasts went well as the DJ hurried to retrieve the mic. Bride's mom reached out and grabbed the mic from the MOH before the DJ could stop her. She got about three words out before the bride jumped from her chair and the photographer grabbed the mic from Mom's hands. It was a close call, but we shut her down. The bride pulled her mother aside and told her to behave herself and that she was not going to make a toast. As a mother, it's sad to see a relationship so damaged between mother and daughter.

Another time I literally grabbed the mic from the bride's aunt. We had gone through the lists of toasts and two additional guests asked if they could give a toast. I told them that time was short, but I would check with the bride and groom. They approved the groom's aunt but no to the bride's aunt. The groom's aunt gave her short, very nice toast, and I was walking back to the DJ with the mic when the bride's aunt approached and reached for the mic. I told her I was sorry, but we didn't have the time for another toast. She began screaming at me that the groom's aunt had toasted so why couldn't she? I had no right to keep her from speaking. I walked away. At the end of the night when everyone was leaving, she told me off again. You would think I would have thicker skin by now.

One night the groom's uncle came to me and asked if he could make a toast to the groom. We were just finishing the toasts and the main course was coming out. I told him I would check with the groom and let him know. When I spoke with the groom, he said he would rather not have his uncle speak, that his uncle tended to embellish and would talk for hours if we let him. I told the uncle that we just didn't have time but maybe later in the evening. The uncle then went to the groom to ask again. My groom was very cool and told him that he would love to have his uncle speak, but that his bossy coordinator would not allow it. I am more than glad to take the blame. I never have to see these would-be toasters again, but my couples do. So, to keep family ties intact, feel free to blame me.

Too many toasts can be as painful as bad toasts. There is only so much time at a wedding reception for dinner, toasts, and dancing. Our couples should want to maximize their time by keeping toasts to a limited number of guests, and to a limited amount of time – three or four minutes each. We suggest that our couples never do an open mic where the mic is passed from guest to guest.

One couple had forty-five minutes of toasts with eighteen different people giving toasts. The DJ, photographer and I counted the toasts and the time spent. Many of the guests wanted to dance and approached me and the DJ asking when dancing would start. Other guests were wandering around the room, eye rolling, and going to the bar for more drinks. I approached the bride and groom and told them that they had one hour left for dancing. I asked if they wanted to cut off the toasts. No, they were fine and wanted to give everyone a chance to say something. What we find, however, is the toasters seem to say the same thing. They thank the bride, groom, and parents for a wonderful night, and how much they love the couple, etc. When the toasts were finally done, this couple was dismayed that there was not much dance time left. I always remind my couples of the time so the evening doesn't get away from them. I try to allow time

for two hours of dancing, but if couples choose to visit and not dance, that's fine too. I just want them to enjoy the evening and visit with guests but still have dance time.

I did a wedding at a private winery for the best friend and college buddy of the winery owner. The wedding was to take place at the top of a hill; cocktail hour, dinner, and dancing poolside in the back of the winery. It was a beautiful setting. We had to have the hill bulldozed to flatten it enough for the chairs to sit evenly. We had to have grass planted as well. The ceremony site had such a steep road that we hired a twenty-four passenger shuttle to take guests up and down. Overall this event was a pricey endeavor for the winery owner and the groom. Because the groom had invited so many of his college buddies, he had a long list of friends to give toasts. Some of these guys accompanied these toasts with short and not-so-short videos. Dinner was to be served at seven o'clock, then eight o'clock came and toasts were still going. The guests were also getting toasted. The caterer was distressed that dinner was getting overdone and they would also be going into overtime, since they were scheduled out by ten o'clock. I approached the groom for the third or fourth time letting him know that dinner was waiting. But no, these were his buddies and the toasts would continue. The hell with dinner. Dinner was finally served at nine o'clock and hopefully enjoyed by those that could still taste it. The caterers finally cleaned up and left well into overtime.

I finished my part of the evening, and most of the guests had left or were leaving by shuttle. The groom and his buddies continued to party and open wine from the wine cellar. The photographer stayed on for another hour. The next morning I got a call from the photographer; I missed all the excitement. After I left the bride's father, trying to keep up with the groom and guys, had fallen down the stairs to the wine cellar and broke his ankle. In hindsight, some of these toasts and videos could have been done at the rehearsal dinner. Couples need to think about their guests too, and too many toasts can be just that: too many toasts.

I think the *pièce de résistance* was the night that the lady sang—not the "fat lady." We were welcoming guests to this winery wedding and sparkling wine was being served as guests arrived. A couple in their mid-sixties arrived and asked if they were late for the Smith wedding. I said no, but this wedding was the Jones wedding. I told her that she must be at the wrong venue and if she would show me her invitation I would be glad to give her instructions to her winery wedding. She didn't have an invitation. The couple had called in the last minute invitation and she was sure she was at the right place. I again asked her the name of the couple and she gave me another name that was not the name of my couple. The winery manager and I told her and her husband that this was a private event and that they should leave the premises. But to be sure, I got their name and checked my guest list. Yes, their name was on the list. Even if they didn't know the name of the bride and groom, they had been invited and they would stay. When the musicians started to play music for the procession, this lady came up to me and asked if she could sing. I said no, that we were fine with what the bride and groom had planned.

The ceremony and cocktail hour went off well, and then guests were invited in for dinner. The bride and groom entered, did their first dance, and then were seated at their Sweetheart table for the welcome toast and then dinner service. All was going smoothly as the first course came out. When it was time for the toasts, the DJ prepped the toasters and cued the photographer that we were ready. The toasts began. Our little lady friend came to me during the toasts and asked if she could sing. I said no, we have a small list of those giving toasts, but thanks anyway. She then went to the DJ and asked if she could give just a short toast, and he also told her no, but would check with the groom to make sure that she hadn't been missed on the list.

When the DJ asked the groom, he replied that she was a distant cousin so maybe just a quick word to keep her happy. The next thing I knew this woman had the mic in her hand and was singing "Ave Maria." Oh my God, it was awful and off key. I went over to the DJ and said, "What the hell? I told you she was not to make a toast, not sing!"

The DJ stated laughing, "Darlene, you should see your face. It's hilarious." She sang every word and all the verses. The guests laughed, the bride and groom were startled, and I was pissed. She had gotten her way and gotten in her song. The groom later apologized and told us that she had always been a little odd. Odd? Really? Now whenever that DJ wants to get to me he says, "I think I'll sing 'Ave Maria.'"

Word to brides and groom: be discerning when choosing who may and who may not make toasts. I am glad to take the blame. If you don't want to hurt a family member, friend or guest by refusing them, just blame it on me. "Darlene says we don't have time, otherwise we would love to have you make the toast." I have taken the blame more than once and am glad to again.

Chapter 19:

Challenging Brides, To Say the Least

I HAVE DONE OVER TWENTY-FIVE HUNDRED WEDDINGS in these thirty-five years and less than a handful have been difficult. Sometimes it's not the bride or groom but their families. In the early years, I put up with it. I was not really sure how to deal with them and didn't want to hurt any feelings. Hopefully I've gotten better, or maybe just tougher, although I have times when I still come home in tears. I tell my couples that I run a tight ship, especially with vendors because I want my weddings to be flaw-less. My couples are my first priority, and the vendors need be courteous and professional. I have been called "sergeant" by some of my groomsmen, and I take this as a compliment.

I can count the very difficult and not-so-nice brides on one hand. Maybe these difficult brides expect perfection, or have unreasonable ex-pectations, I'm not sure, but it can be exhausting for all concerned.

One bride who was expecting the perfect night threw a fit when she was walking down the aisle. All had gone perfectly and we had a trio play-ing the music. Just as the bride got to the top of the stairs to process down the aisle, we heard some loud music coming from a neighboring home some fifty yards away. I'm not sure the guests could hear it since they were in a more enclosed area, but the bride and her father could hear it. She stopped right where she was and said, "Stop that damn music! I'm not moving until it stops!" I ran over to the musicians and motioned them to loop it and keep playing. I then ran towards the neighboring house. Jim was standing close by and I yelled, "Get over to that house and stop that damn music! The bride won't budge! Move it!" Jim and the security guard ran to the house and spoke to the owner that was having some sort of a party. "Could you please just stop your music for twenty minutes? We are having a wedding next door." The neighbor did begrudgingly stop the music for the next twenty-five minutes, and the bride walked and we continued on. To be honest these neighbors seem to have a lot of parties. At the end of the night, the bride came to me and the winery event manager and told us that we had ruined her wedding. The winery should have notified all the neighbors that there was to be a wedding, and they should have arranged their party for another night. We explained that we cannot control noise whether it's the neighbors, fire trucks, car noise, etc. The winery can only control what happens on their property. It was unfortunate, but we were able to stop the music. Once the guests were inside the winery, we could no longer hear any music coming from anywhere. When you do an outside wedding occasionally you will hear a fire truck, ambulance, or a motorcycle, but we can only control what we can control. I felt bad that our bride was so upset over this very brief interruption, but sometimes you just have to roll with it.

My toughest bride (or I should say meanest bride) was about six years ago. She and her family were from the East Coast. They had been referred to me and we agreed to meet about nine months before the wedding and spend three days meeting with desired vendors, florists, photographers, musicians, DJs, cakes, rehearsal dinner site, etc. The bride came with her parents; the groom was out of the country in the military. From the first minute I met her, I knew she was trouble. She told me the minute we met that this was her wedding, and that it would be the way she wanted it to be, period.

I said, "Okay, we'll do our very best to make sure that happens." She and her parents rode in our car with Jim and I. My first hint of trouble was the bride was so rude and mean to her mother. She would tell her to shut up, f—k up, etc. Mom would just respond, "Now Sue, you don't mean that." If one of my daughters said that to me I would be shocked, pissed, and would respond in kind. Not that my daughters haven't expressed some strong language to me in the past, but not in public.

This wonderful behavior continued throughout the next few days. The cake tasting went wrong. She likes canned cake frosting and why can't the bakers use canned frosting instead of the gooey stuff they use for filling? One of my favorite bakers took me aside and told me this request was insulting. She said she would not use canned frosting. So off we went to another baker. The third baker finally agreed to make a heavier frosting; not canned, but thicker than the buttercream that she would normally use. I again apologized for my bride's behavior. Cake down, moving on.

We met with two photographers that the bride had requested. I had warned them that she was difficult and to be on their toes. The first photographer was too nice and too sensitive, and I was worried for him. They did not gel and thank God, she chose the second photographer who has a thicker skin. I knew he could handle her when the chips were down.

Next, on to meet the florist. The bride wanted all the bells and whistles, draping, lighting, etc. so I had suggested meeting with my favorite, and I consider the most talented designer. He's a great guy and not easily ruffled. However, she got to him to. The flowers had to be this size, this color, and perfectly shaped, even if they had to be cut and dyed. She had a theme in mind of woodsy, yet elegant. She wanted the florist to make the cake stand and the table arrangements in a natural light tree bark. The florist showed her samples of bark that he could order, but no, that's not what she wanted. She had a picture she had cut out of a magazine and what she wanted had to match. What our ingenious florist came up with after ordering several different bark samples was an Aspen bark wrap around that came by the yard. It was bark shaved off a tree and was thin enough to glue to a cake stand, centerpiece etc. It was light enough to easily move and set up. Bride Sue approved and our florist ordered it. This was glued around the wooden cake stand and the wooden box centerpieces. I thought it was brilliant.

The live musicians were hired, a very professional trio, and my favorite DJ rounded out the team. The officiant would be a friend of the bride and groom's. We made room blocks at one of our local and very nice hotels and found a small, elegant restaurant for the rehearsal dinner, so were we set. While the bride was looking at rehearsal dinner spots, she and her parents had tried a very nice restaurant in the Valley, but even though she liked the food, she said the server was too slow and needed to be fired. In fact, she was going to blog him in the hopes that the restaurant would fire him. I asked her if she does this often, and told her that was a bit harsh. She then told me that she will blog and take down anyone that didn't meet her expectations. I joked that I hoped she was kidding and to leave me out of her blogging. To be honest, all of her vendors were afraid of her by the time she left town.

I would have loved to quit this wedding, but I had signed a contract, and actually, I was afraid of her blogging skills. Unfortunately, too many people are willing to damage someone's life and reputation.

The day of the rehearsal arrived, and I got to meet the young groom. He was so nice! What was he doing with her? I noticed that the bridal party said yes to the bride a lot. They were also younger than most of my wedding parties. I would say in their early twenties. The rehearsal went okay with the bride telling her mother off through most of the afternoon. The bride's father never corrected the bride's bad behavior.

The bride also told me that she wanted a sparkler send off. When I told her that sparklers are not legal in our county due to the chance of wildfires, she said, "No one will know, and we'll do it anyway." I again said no, that we wouldn't and couldn't have fire, period.

The day of the wedding, the weather was great and we were ready, or so I hoped. Jim and I got to the winery early to make sure all was in good shape. The centerpieces were amazing with their aspen finish. The room and table set ups were beautiful. There could be no complaints; everything was perfect.

The bride and her party arrived, and the bride was complaining that her hair and make-up were not exactly as she wanted, although she had brought her hair and make-up artist with her from the East. She continued to complain throughout the photos about the heat, the angle of the sun, and anything else she could think of. The photographer and his assistant held on and were counting the hours until the end. The ceremony went well, and the cocktail hour was in full swing when the bride pulled me aside in a snit and said that the signature cocktail that she had ordered was not right. She had asked for Champagne or in California, sparkling wine, poured in a flute with a touch of raspberry. puree. The caterer, in order to serve one hundred and fifty guests, had put the puree in the bottom of the flute, so all they had to do was pour the sparking over the puree. Guests could have the sparkling plain if they chose. The bride was upset; she wanted the puree poured on top of each glass as it was filled and not on the bottom.

I pulled the caterer over to talk to the bride, and the caterer told her that in order to serve this many guests, they had to pre-pour the puree. The taste and color is the same if it's on the bottom or the top, it's still amazing and beautiful. Our bride was still furious. "I told you I want what I want; now pour it on the top."

Dinner went well, dancing started and I thought, *we're going to make it.* I was packing up gifts and leftover items for the family to take at the end of the night when the bride came up to me and asked when I was setting up the sparklers. I told her I wasn't, that I had checked again with the winery and they are not allowed, county ordinance. Sue then went over to her carryon and pulled out one hundred and fifty sparklers and told me to make sure the guests had them for the sendoff. She could care less what the ordinance was.

At that moment the bride's mother walked in and I explained the situation again. Her mother, bless her, was firm this time and said that she had to support the winery in this instance. Sue continued to pout that we were ruining her perfect day. I talked to her photographer and the winery manager, and we came up with a compromise. The photographer would light two sparklers, take the couple outside for photos, and the couple could wave the sparkers in the photos and the guests were not included. No damage done and she had her damn sparklers. We survived the night, thanked the bride, and hugged her mother. What that poor woman puts up with. I watched Yelp for months after that to make sure all had survived her wrath. I often wonder if the marriage survived. To this day the florist and I talk about the wedding from hell.

A wedding I did maybe thirty years ago was the groom, not the bride, that was difficult. He was very sweet and was always kind, but he wore me out. He planned the entire wedding himself. He and the bride were both engineers and the bride was actually his boss. The ceremony, dinner, and dancing would be held outside in a resort in Sonoma, also in the wine country.

I met with the groom six months in advance to start the planning. He had picked the menu, photographer, florist, and all other vendors. The guest list was seventy-five or so, and an afternoon wedding on a beautiful patio. The groom had picked the bridesmaids' dresses and the groomsmen tuxedos. I still remember the wedding colors since we discussed them in such detail.

My groom was a worrier, and he called me every single day with updates. Three weeks before, the bridesmaids' dresses weren't in, two weeks before, the matching gloves for the BM weren't in. Was I sure about the table set up? Did we have enough programs? I kept telling him it was going to be fine, we were in good shape.

At the rehearsal I thought we were going to have to give him Valium, he was that nervous. The bride, a beautiful little woman that I had never met until that day, was very calm. She told me she had planned the honeymoon and the rest was up to the groom. He was a planner and she wasn't.

The day of the wedding everyone looked wonderful. The bridesmaid dresses with the long, matching gloves were outstanding. Our groom should be a designer. The flowers in the same soft colors matched the napkins. Everything was beautiful. Just before the couple was scheduled to walk down the aisle, my groom told me he was going to faint or throw up or both, and we had to sit him down and delay for fifteen minutes until he calmed down. I held his hand and tried to calm him. I was beginning to feel like his mother. How could I get my poor new son down the aisle? Would be need a chair at the altar to sit down? I told the groomsmen to stay close in case he went down.

He did make it through the ceremony, and we were ready for the reception. . Get this guy a glass of wine and let dinner begin. He did okay through dinner and the toasts even though his color was a bit ashen. After dinner during dancing, which he made it through, I had a chance to speak to his mother. She asked, "How bad was it?"

"I'm sorry," I told her, "What do you mean?"

She said again, "How bad was it? How bad was he? Did he drive you nuts? He's a worrier. He came out of the womb a worrier. I love him to death but he wears me out."

I totally understood what she was saying, because yes, he wore me out too, but I had also grown fond of him. At the end of the night I did dance with our groom. I don't normally dance at my weddings either, although at times I am tempted. But that's another story.

When we danced I told him what a nice guy he was and how he would make a great dad, but that he needed to calm down before he killed himself or someone else. He laughed, and we kept in touch for the next year with cards and the occasional phone call.

I almost fired one demanding bride over her constant calls and changes. She would call on a Saturday morning and tell me, not ask me, to meet her at the venue. She wanted to show it to her friend or photographer or wanted me to look at this color sample to see if it would look good with the linens, etc. After three or four times of these last minute demands, I told her that I didn't think that we were a good fit. I had other brides and I couldn't drop everything each time she wanted an unscheduled meeting.

Even I have a life. Well, sort of. I would be glad to give her a refund and help her find another coordinator. Within an hour, she called back, apologized, and said she would behave. She turned out to be a wonderful bride and never pushed again. We had a great relationship by the time the big day arrived. Note to brides: please be respectful of your vendors. They have feelings too.

Rain has also caused brides to lose it. We do remind them when they plan a winter wedding it may rain or be very cold. If it rains we can usually move the ceremony inside. We try to give ourselves two hours before the ceremony to call if we need to move inside. If the chairs get wet, it takes time for them to dry, and if they have fabric on the chairs, forget it; they'll be soaked all night. So we watch the weather closely. One bride insisted that she was going to have her wedding outside, and we set up the chairs outside. An hour before the ceremony it started to rain, and I told the staff to move the chairs inside. We set about making the inside beautiful with extra candles, lanterns, and flowers. The florist and the whole team pitched in. We have done this move many times, and we are comfortable with this last minute change. I told the bride that it was raining and that we had moved the ceremony inside. She started crying, "My wedding is being ruined." I talked to the groom and he was fine with moving inside and the bride would get over it. We moved the chairs inside and finished the set up. Thirty minutes before the ceremony, the rain was lightening up, and the bride demanded that we move the chairs back outside.

So the staff jumped back in and we moved the chairs back out. The staff was not happy, they had other things to do, but oh well, the bride is always right. Yep, the minute that the ceremony started, the downpour also started. The guests were soaked in minutes. The guests moved under alcoves and eaves to the side of the ceremony. The couple was under an overhang so they were dry. As soon as the ceremony was over, we moved the cocktail hour to an upstairs tasting room, small but doable, and went back to finishing off the room for dining. The chair cushions had to be towel dried and never completely dried. The caterers had scrambled to move the cocktail hour inside and serve the guests wine and appetizers in a timely manner. Everyone worked their butts off, and we felt really good about our quick turnaround. Our Bride was still sobbing when she entered the room for dinner, that her day was not the perfect one she had planned. When you plan a winter wedding, you should have a rain plan.

Another wedding where it rained, the couple handled it much differently. It was a Jewish ceremony with a chuppah at the altar. A chuppah is normally a cloth covering for the bride, groom, and rabbi to stand under. The chuppah had been set up and decorated by the florist several hours before. It was beautiful. When it started to rain, the couple agreed to move everything inside. However, the chuppah, which was on four poles, was too tall to get through the doors and would hit the lighting fixtures in the barrel room. Finally with the help of the florist, Jim, and two groomsmen, they turned the chuppah on its side and then got it in. Our DJ climbed up on a ladder to hold back the chandeliers so that the towering chuppah would not break the chandeliers. The florist and our helpers were able to transform the barrel room into a a lovely ceremony site, with the guest chairs facing the altar and chuppah. All the dining tables were pushed to one side and the room darkened so that the tables were no longer visible.

The legs of the chuppah were not as steady as they would be outside attached to pillars, so four members of our bridal party stood holding onto the legs of the chuppah, and it looked like it had been planned. Even our rabbi was impressed. The ceremony went well and afterward, when we were quickly flipping the room, we found that we would not have time to get the chuppah back out again, nor did we want to get it wet. So our ingenious florist took off the covering of the chuppah and put barrels around the legs with lanterns and candles on the barrels. This left an arch and opening for the caterers to enter through from the kitchen. It also was a pretty back drop for dancing. It no longer looked like a chuppah. They say when you are given lemons, you make lemonade. The bride and groom were very happy and pleased with the team effort.

Suggestion: if you are having a winter wedding where it could rain or be very cold, think of alternatives and have a backup plan. If it's cold but clear, think about providing pashminas or throws for the back of the chairs. These can be favors for your guests in your wedding colors. Think about having hot cider on guest arrival or maybe hot chocolate instead of infused water. Make sure your venue has sufficient outdoor and indoor heating. You might want to have a propane fire pit outside for guests to enjoy later.

☙❧

As I have mentioned, we have had wonderful, easygoing brides and have had brides a little more difficult. I need to know that I can work with a bride, but the bride also needs to feel comfortable working with me. It's a two way street, and if it's not going to work, we should part ways early on in the process.

Some years ago, I had this sweet couple with special needs. They were so gentle and so in love with each other that they melted the hearts of all the vendors. One of my favorite photographers came to me before the wedding, and he whispered that the two had a special language just between the two of them. So I listened carefully during the ceremony, and true enough, when they spoke to each other it was almost a code language that only the two of them could understand. This was one ceremony that did bring tears to the guests and the vendors. At the end of the night when they were leaving, I asked them how they were getting back to their hotel up the road. They told me that they were walking. They were both still dressed for the wedding, she in her gown and he in his tux, but added to the back of his tux was a sign: "Just Married." Off they went, walking in the dark up the highway. About ten minutes later, a highway patrolman stopped by the winery and asked me about the couple walking up the road. He asked if I thought they were ok. He had offered them a ride to their hotel, maybe a mile away. He was worried about them getting hit by a car in the dark. I told him that I thought they would be okay, but they were very proud and wanted to show off their "Just Married" sign.

I had one couple that left on the back of a Harley Davidson bike. The bride wrapped her gown around her legs, put on her helmet, and off they went. That's what makes this business so interesting—there is always diversity.

෨෮

We had one couple that we met with that, within minutes, I knew I could not work with the groom. He came across as not only arrogant but downright rude. He told us how he and his future wife saw the day going. He would ask me a question, but before I could answer, he would hold up his hand and to stop me. He would continue on with his rules, and how he was in charge, etc. The bride let him do most of the talking. Later I met with the venue onsite coordinator, and she told me that the groom had been very rude to her. Whenever she mentioned something about their rules or her experience in the matter, he would tell her to stop and actually put his hand on her mouth to silence her. She said she would refuse to be on site the day of the wedding and someone else from the venue could handle him.

I told Jim that I could not work with him and had Jim send him an email that I was no longer available for their date. He did have his wedding with another male coordinator. Sometimes you know right from the start that you're not a good fit, and it's time to bow out.

Two years or so ago, we did fire a bride. She was holding her wedding in the winter at a resort hotel. When she called to hire us upon recommendation, she tried to get us to lower our prices. I think we are very reasonable with three different packages the bride and groom can choose from. I have been told that I don't charge enough. But this one bride was persistent and told me that this other coordinator was less money than I was. I told her then hire the other coordinator; I was not going to lower my price.

She then told me that she was doing so much of the work and that I wouldn't need to do much. Yeah, yeah, I've heard that before. These brides normally want more, not less. A week later this bride called me and said she really wanted to hire us. We agreed to meet at the venue in the next few weeks. I always ask to meet and walk the venue to see the bride's vision and where all the set ups will be: ceremony, cocktail, dinner, and dancing. We also scheduled the meeting with the resort coordinator.

The bride went over her vision, which was very elaborate and would take hours of set up. The difficult part of this plan was the limited time frame. We could not get in to set up until four hours before, but the set up would take six to seven hours with at least four people working on it. This was not a set up that the florist would be doing. It actually needed a professional decorating crew.

The bride gave me a list of the vendors that she had hired, and I called several of them to go over the details. I called the bride after these conversations to discuss hiring a décor crew for this time consuming set up. I told her I would be glad to hire a crew, but she would need to pay for the crew. I don't get on ladders and hang fabric or lighting from the ceiling. I am also not a florist, but I have contacts that could do these things. After several meetings with her, it became apparent that she didn't want to hire anyone and expected us to do all of the set up and décor. Even if we were willing to climb on ladders and put up all this décor, there just was not time in the small window the venue allowed. When she told me that I should pay for these outside vendors myself, I said we were done. I told her that I was sending back her deposit and I recommended several other coordinators. I suggest that brides should be realistic when they hire their vendors. Your florist doesn't cook or get the bridal party down the aisle. Your photographer doesn't make cakes and move tables. Each vendor is professional in their own way. I am always glad to help with any set ups that I can—move a flower arrangement or set up a dessert table. I can't hang lighting or take photos. You want and deserve the best, so hire the best.

☙❧

There have been very few times when collecting our balance was difficult. We expect the balance two weeks before the wedding, as do most vendors. Most all of our couples respect this. In my earlier days it was awkward for me, and I didn't really like to ask for the balance. I still don't enjoy it, but once the wedding is over, there is no reason to pay the balance. Once the food is eaten, there is no reason to pay the caterer. Only the photographer can withhold the photos.

For one of my early weddings, I did not ask for the balance until the end of the night, and then I was told that they would pay me when they got back from their honeymoon. I'm sure by the time they got back they wouldn't have the money to pay me. So I asked where they were staying and I would follow them to their hotel so they could get their checkbook. I did and they paid me.

One wedding five or six years ago, I had sent a reminder of the balance and I asked if they would please send a check. I don't like to bring up money at the rehearsal and never the day of the wedding. I got a response from the groom; the check is in the mail. Okay, fine. The night of the rehearsal, I asked again for the check and the groom told me that they had paid the balance several weeks ago. Okay, I will check with my bank, thank you. In these times you can easily access your bank account, so when I got home I went into my bank account and there was no record of a check being received. I also make a notation in my checkbook and Jim tracks it on the computer, so we were sure that we hadn't been paid.

The next day before the wedding, I quietly mentioned to the groom that we had not received the check and would need to collect before the end of the night. He assured me that he would take care of it, and the day proceeded on. I spoke with the DJ and asked if he had been paid the balance and he said no, he would ask after the wedding. The photographer also said no, but he could withhold the photos if he was not paid. The caterers had been paid by the bride's parents..

At the end of the night when all the guests had left and the bride, groom, and family were carrying out the gifts, I approached the groom again and reminded him of the final balance. He told me that the check must still be in the mail. I then told him that I would be glad to take a new check and when and if the other check arrived, I would immediately send the first check back. No problem. But no, he was not going to give me a check. He thought I was questioning his integrity. The groom's mother walked over and said she was glad to give me a check for the balance and he could reimburse her. His mother did proceed to give me a check and I assured both of them that I would send the other check back the minute I received it.

An hour later, Jim and I had helped with clean up and were on our way home. The groom called me on my cell phone, yelling at me that I had ruined his wedding by asking for payment and that the bride's entire night had been ruined. I reminded him that I didn't even mention the money until the guests were gone and never had approached the bride. Well, I had embarrassed him in front of his Mother, etc. I was heartbroken, and I cried all the way home and most of the night. The evening had been so nice and the bride so happy, why did it have to be ruined? The DJ told me the next week that he had never been paid, nor had the photographer. The missing check never did show up. All this heartbreak could have been avoided.

The very worst money situation that I ever witnessed was maybe four years ago. My heart broke for the bride and groom. We had been hired by the bride and groom but told that the bride's family was responsible for the payments to vendors. No problem, the bride and groom paid me the initial deposit. I had not received the balance by the day of the rehearsal, so I mentioned it to the bride. She said her mother was handling it, and when I spoke to her mother she gave me a check for the balance with a tip included. How nice, thank you so much.

The next day during the ceremony, the caterer came to me and told me that they had not been paid and unless they were paid, they could not serve dinner. Once the meal is over, there is no reason to pay the caterer. Apparently the caterer had received a check two weeks prior from the bride's family and the check had bounced. They put the check through again, and it bounced again. The day before they had asked for a credit card and it was declined, and then a second card was declined. Could Jim or I ask the groom or bride's family for a new card, or what would they prefer we do?

I was busy with the cocktail hour so Jim approached the family. They told him to take it up with the best man or the groom. Well, who wants to ruin someone's wedding? Jim went to the best man and told him the situation. He told Jim don't tell the bride or groom. He would handle it. The best man spoke to the bride's father, who said to talk to his wife, and she said it had been taken care of. However it had not been taken care of. Jim went back to the caterer, and she told us that she had to have a credit card before they could serve the meal. We were then forty minutes from meal service.

Jim went back to the best man, and he went to the other groomsmen and bridal party and collected credit cards from all of them, sixteen to be exact. So dinner was paid for and the meal was served. At one point the groom came to me and asked if everything was okay. "Absolutely, everything is going beautifully." I may go to hell someday for lying. In the meantime the best man had to give his toast, and he told Jim and I that he was having a hard time concentrating, between collecting credit cards and taking notes of how much he owed back to whom, and trying to keep this from the bride and groom.

The bride came to me halfway through dinner and asked that her mother be cut off from all wine service since she was potted. I went by her table, and yes, she was being taken out for air by her husband. The groom then approached and asked what was going on; he had noticed his groomsmen walking around with a fistful of credit cards. I gave him a hug and said, "I'm so sorry, but you probably should speak to your best man."

By this time, I just wanted the night to be over. The groom now knew the truth, the bride's mom was drunk, and we were all trying to keep the bride in the dark, so to speak. The night, however, did continue and the guests enjoyed the dancing. It took the caterer an hour to run all the credit cards. Finally by the end of the night, the groom had told the bride, and the bride's mom had been taken back to the hotel, blissfully unaware of all the chaos she had created. Did her husband care? Who knows? Both the bride and groom were in tears as they said goodnight and how sorry they were that they had caused all these problems. We gave them a hug and told them we were so sorry, and they hadn't created any problems and don't let it ruin your night. As if it wasn't already ruined. The best man told us later that the bride's mom has a little drinking problem and had actually gone to the rental house where the bridal party was staying and had consumed all the liquor when the bridal party was out sightseeing and wine tasting. My biggest question at the end of the night was why the bride's dad put up with it or let his wife deal with the wedding money? He could have told the bride and groom in the beginning that they couldn't afford the expense of the wedding. Why wait until the night of the wedding and put the couple and everyone else involved through such humiliation? Ah, family dynamics, who knows?

Just a footnote to the story: the check we received from bride's mom bounced, as did the checks the DJ and the photographer received. The groom compensated all of us and the kind best man and guests that had put up their credit cards. What an expensive and heartbreaking night.

It's not always the bride or family that can be difficult or mean—it can also be the bridal party or guests. One of our bridesmaids who was also the groom's sister got very drunk before she arrived at the rehearsal. Apparently she had been doing a bit of wine tasting. During the rehearsal on the lawn she could not stand up or make it down the aisle. She kicked off her shoes, almost hitting another bridesmaid, and literally fell over twice, once holding the three-year-old flower girl. I could not get her to pay attention or even stand in her position. I told the bride it was hopeless and we should just practice without her. We left her sitting on the lawn saying she was going to be sick. The bride was furious, and I thought she was going to punch her, but she only called her names and said how sorry she was that she was going to be her sister in law. The next day at the wedding she was fine. I didn't even recognize her when she was cleaned up and sober.

One of my grooms almost ended up in jail for his wedding with a DUI charge. The day of the rehearsal the bridal party arrived on time for the wedding rehearsal, but no bride and groom. I went over the line up with the party until the bride arrived in tears. It seemed that the groom had been arrested right in front of the winery where the wedding was to be held. The highway patrol had him out front walking a white line and taking a breathalyzer test. The couple had been wine tasting up valley, and when the groom drove past the winery for the rehearsal, he made an illegal U turn on a busy highway, and busted, a highway patrol officer was right there.

I couldn't get the bride to pay any attention, so we decided to hold off the rehearsal to see what happened with the groom. One of the groomsmen went out to the highway to intervene. An hour or so later, the groom did make it to the rehearsal. The officer gave our groom a ticket and a warning but did not haul him off. Since he was getting married the officer had shown a soft heart and let it go this time. The rehearsal went well but late, and the groom was terribly embarrassed. The wedding went well the next day with much teasing to the groom about almost missing his wedding by being in jail. The parents had not heard the story and were horrified. The bride's dad said, "My God, my daughter is marrying a jailbird or a lush."

We'd have a few catfights between the bride and the bridesmaids the day of the wedding. Sometimes it is obvious that jealousy is the culprit. Sometimes the girls don't like their dresses or the other girls. One such bridesmaid didn't like the dress and really didn't want to be in the wedding, so she came the day of the wedding in a wrinkled dress and no makeup. We had offered to steam all the dresses, but this bridesmaid had refused. The bride was very upset with the bridesmaid and asked her why she was doing this to her on her big day. The bridesmaid told her, "I told you. I don't like the Groom. You made a bad choice, and I may have to be in it, but I don't have to enjoy it." The bride then told her she could leave if she wanted, and so she did. One down. Who needs her anyway?

The groomsmen may be ill behaved at the rehearsal, sassing back or drinking too much, but the day of the wedding, they're usually the best behaved. I can count on my guys to perform their best. We did have one groomsman last summer that fainted during the ceremony. It was hot, and he locked his knees and down he went. Photographer reached over, grabbed him, and put him in a chair in the front row. Jim, as the officiant, carried on, and the bridal party walked out together, one groomsman short.

At the end of one night there was a standoff over the leftover beer. The couple had ordered beer in kegs, obviously more beer than they needed. A five-gallon keg will serve fifty or so glasses. A fifteen-gallon keg will serve one hundred and fifty or so guests. This couple had purchased more beer than they needed. At the end of the night, there was at least half a keg left. One of the groomsmen walked into the bar area as we were cleaning up and told me that he was taking the leftover keg. I told him, "I'm sorry, but the keg belongs to the property and you can't take the keg. You can provide us with containers and we'll gladly pour the beer into the containers."

"No," he said, "I'm coming back there behind the bar and I'm taking the keg. I'll return it tomorrow."

I said, "You are not coming behind the bar, and you're not taking the keg." He then told me he was a lawyer and he could sue me. "Okay," I said, "Sue me. But you're not coming back here," and I told the poor young caterer manning the bar to go get security because we were obviously going to have a fight on our hands. The groomsman finally left, muttering that he would see me in court. Yeah, yeah, I've heard that before too. God, I'm really turning into a hard ass. What fun!

We have also taken car keys away if a guest is not fit to drive. This does not happen often, and most of the time it's because the guest started drinking earlier in the day. One night it was obvious that this guest was not capable of driving, so Jim asked for his keys and told him that we would get a taxi. This was before Uber or Lyft. The gentleman said, "No, I'm fine." He was not fine, so Jim followed him out to the parking lot and tried again to get the key. The man jumped in his car and proceeded to peel out of the parking lot. Oops! He hit two trees, and he had to leave the car to head out on foot. Fortunately, another guest cornered him and loaded him in his car. The next morning a tow truck picked up the car. The trees were another matter and needed some serious propping up. Most venues have a policy of insurance to cover these damages to property. Now I know why.

Another night, one of the guests literally scared the wits out of us. I was alone with the winery staff and we were locking up and ready to go. The lights had just been turned off and we were walking out when a gentleman came out of the dark and asked where everyone had gone. "Ah, they left about an hour ago." We had a shuttle to take the guests back to their hotels in Napa.

"So can you call me a taxi?" In this small town there is not a taxi service, and he would be here alone in the dark when we left. The security guard was very kind and offered to take him back to his hotel. It seemed that the gentlemen had gone outside and fallen asleep on a bench and wasn't aware when the others left.

A month later both the winery employee and I received a twenty-five-dollar gift card from Steve, the young man that had been sleeping outside. Some good deeds do not go unnoticed. I now count heads and double check before the shuttle leaves.

Besides the brides, I would say the bride's mother can be one of the worst offenders, and thank goodness we have had very few of these. Décor planned by the bride or mom has been the problem a few times. Some venues provide the linens and at some venues, we have to rent the linens. We know what size linens fit what size tables, and we share this with the bride, family and the caterer. Once in a while the bride or her mother would like to provide the linens. One such mother insisted that she would make all the linens for the tables. We gave her the measurements, and she had four months to complete her project. The day of the rehearsal, the bride's mother gave us the linens. Oh, my. Well, they did look homemade. The seams were crooked and when on the tables, the linens did not reach the floor. If we pushed the chairs in close, maybe the linen length won't be noticed. Of course mom was upset, and we must have given her the wrong size for the tables, or we had switched tables, but this couldn't be her fault. She's an expert seamstress. Yes, I've heard this before too, but we had to fix this mess. The florist added more greenery and candles to the table so that the guest's eye would draw to the top of the table and not to the length. Hopefully the guests would sit down quickly, and if we kept the room dark, the guests would not notice that the linens were crooked and too short.

One mother insisted on being present when the bride and groom did their "first look" photos. The first look is normally just the bride and groom. The photographer captures the moment when they see each other before the wedding for the first time. It's a very special, *private* moment. This mother told me that she had to be back there and that her daughter would want her there. I said I would check with the photographer and let her know if she was wanted or needed back there. "How dare you insult me or question me? Of course my daughter wants me there, now get out of my way." Back she went. I forgot to ask if she was invited on the honeymoon.

Another groom's sister pulled the same line. The photographer had been given a list of family photos and who was to be in them. The photographer had the family on the lawn after the ceremony, calling members up as they were needed for the photos. The groom's sister came up to me and asked when her family would have photos with the bride and groom. I went to check with the photographer, and he didn't have them on the list but would make room for them at the end of his list. When I told the sister this, she called me a liar and a bitch. She said that I was keeping her out of the photos. I'm not sure why I would do this since I didn't know her, but okay, it must be my fault. I told her the photographer would come and get her and I walked away.

I have been chewed out more than once. A bride's aunt was upset after looking at the seating chart to find that she was sitting in the back corner of the room, away from the bride and groom. She called me over and demanded that I move her to a table closer to the couple. I showed her the seating chart provided by the bride and assured her that she was at the correct table. "Nonsense, my niece would never do this to me. I'm her favorite aunt! You did this, now move me!"

"I'm sorry," I responded, "but I can't move you. This is what the bride wanted. I will look into this, but now I do have other guests to seat," and I walked away. You just can't make everyone happy all the time.

Another mother refused my and the caterer's suggestion of assigned tables, let alone assigned seating. We explained to her that each guest should be assigned a specific table with their family or friends. Then we know how many chairs to put at each table, place settings, and have the guests name and their meal choice. The guests can pick up their place card, find their table by the table number, and be seated. Then meal service is easy. If the guests have a choice of meal, then the caterers need to know each guest's meal choice at each table. However, this one mother refused; it was way too much work for her. Since all the guests would be receiving the same meal, she saw so need to assign table numbers. We were to put the same amount of chairs at each table and the guests could choose where they wanted to sit. We told her it could lead to a mess, but she would not budge.

The night arrived and after the ceremony when guests started to be seated, it was a mess! A family of ten would grab one table and take chairs from another table. Then another table was short of chairs, and we end up with five people at this table. The groom's family came to me and asked where they were to sit. They had a family of eight and wanted to sit together, but they could not find a table together since most tables had an odd assortment of guests and chairs. The groom's family finally went outside to a patio table and ate by themselves when they should have been inside close to the bride and groom. The bride's mother came to me a bit later and asked why the groom's family was eating outside. I just told her that when they came in from photos, there was no table left for their family. This is why we assign tables. Most all venues now insist on assigned seating.

Some couples often bring too much stuff or décor. That's fine, but please let your coordinator know that you are bringing five, ten, or twenty boxes of décor for your coordinator to put out. Also please give us a list of what you are bringing and where these items are to go. We are glad to put out the place cards, programs, table numbers, pictures, etc., but we need to know where it goes.

One mother told us that she was bringing the centerpieces, simple little china teapots, and the florist would put some greenery around them. The day of the rehearsal she brought twenty-two boxes of china and décor. Thank goodness I had brought my daughter Debbie to help because this was a big property at a local resort, and there is a lot of moving from one area to another. Ceremony on one lawn, cocktail hour on another, dinner on a patio at another location, and finally dancing in the barrel room seventy-five yards away. This venue is beautiful, but there is a lot of footwork.

Well, I'm so glad I brought Debbie. I put her to work setting up the teapots for the centerpieces so the florist could place the greenery. However, it was not one teapot but five pieces on china: several pots, a small tray, and a few cups. These were apparently family treasures. It took Debbie over three hours to set up all of these tables while I put out place cards. After dinner when I took the guests down to the barrel room for dancing, I put Debbie to work again, wrapping and boxing every one of these tea set pieces. Another two hours. She then had to move the boxes to the area where the bride's family could easily load them in their car at the end of the night. These were too heavy for Debbie to lift, so she was able to borrow a kitchen cart from the venue to move the boxes to the load out area. This would take five trips, so while the guests were dancing, I helped Debbie by walking along, holding the boxes so they wouldn't fall off the cart. Instead of having Debbie's help with other tasks, I was doing double duty during dinner and dancing while she was loading and toting.

At the end of the evening, Debbie had all the boxes put on the lawn area for easy load out while I gathered the gifts, flowers, leftover cake, and other items and took them out to the lawn area with the other boxes. After the bride and groom said goodbye to their guests, I mentioned to the bride's mom that everything was boxed and ready for her and her family to load into their vehicles. "What?" she said. "You expect me to load all those boxes? No, I'm sorry. They're way too heavy." She proceeded to bring her car around and park it next to the pile of boxes. She told Debbie and I that she was ready for us to load. And load we did. It took us all of thirty minutes of stuffing, pushing, and rearranging. When we were done, the only space left was the driver's seat. Debbie told me later that she was tempted never to work for me again. She also told me to buy a push cart, which I did. We also bought one for the winery that we work at frequently.

I spoke to another coordinator about this problem of bringing too many unidentified boxes to put out and then box up. She said that she had lost assistants and helpers for this very reason. They spent the whole night packing and unpacking. It's backbreaking work and too often not appreciated. When the families have to take this "stuff" at the end of the night, they're floored. They want us to either ship it to them or hold it for the next day when they're rested. Most if not all venues want all items out at the end of the night. I spell this out in my timelines: all must go at the end of the night. I also ask who will be responsible for these items. I often get an argument at the end of the night, that they don't have the energy to load out all these boxes. Brides, please think about this when you are planning your wedding. What comes in must go out.

We have also found very unusual items left at the end of the night. The caterers have found and turned into me, a prostatic leg and dentures wrapped in a napkin. I can understand the dentures, but how the hell did the guest leave without his or her leg?

Speaking of seating, we had one bride fib about her guest count. We were told seventy-five guests, and we had set up the room, tables, and chairs for seventy-five guests. We had a seating chart and guest list to confirm the seventy-five guests. At the ceremony, the number of guests looked larger than seventy-five and I started counting heads. The caterer noticed the same thing at the cocktail hour, and we counted ninety-four guests. Before we were to seat guests, I mentioned to the bride could we possibly have more guests than seventy-five or did we have some crashers? "Well," the bride said, "I may have invited a few more people that I mentioned, but I wasn't sure that they'd come. Is that a problem?"

"No problem, we'll deal with it," I responded. Okay, now fix the problem. We needed three more tables, three more linens, more china, flatware, glassware, and oh yes, more food.

I went to the caterer, and we set up three more tables and grabbed extra chairs that were provided by the venue. We did not have enough linens, so while the guests were transitioning from the cocktail hour to the dining area, some two hundred feet, we would grab the cocktail table linens and put them on the dinner tables. They would be a little short, but oh well, you make do. We didn't have enough china, but we had paper plates, so we switched those out for the children's tables. One wine glass instead of two, and the tables were ready. For the food, the catering manager and I approached the chef and told him smaller portions and cut the chicken in half if you have to. Just do what you have to do. We made it through the evening just fine. At the end of the night the bride apologized but was not happy when she was given a revised bill for the ninety-four guests instead of the seventy-five. I think her thought was undercount the number and pay less. She didn't think we were going to actually count guests. Well, now you know, all coordinators and caterers do count guests.

Be honest with your vendors and your guests. This also goes for the invitations. If the ceremony starts at six o'clock, then put six o'clock on the invitation. You can include in the invitation a map and a note guest can arrive a half hour early or so. Guests arriving too early are an inconvenience to the venue, vendors, and to guest themselves. There is nothing for them to do when they arrive early, and they often get testy with the staff or with me. One group arrived an hour and a half early for a six o'clock ceremony. When the ceremony did not start an older gentlemen came to me and asked why I was delaying the ceremony. I told him I was sorry but the ceremony was at six o'clock, please be comfortable and we'll start on time. He then showed me the invitation that said five o'clock and called me a liar. I told him I was not the liar, but that the bride and groom had put an earlier time, maybe to give guests extra travel time. He continued to follow me around and harass me until the ceremony actually started on time at six o'clock. Later in the night, he did find me to apologize.

Our couples think that by changing the ceremony time on the invitation they will be assured the guests are on time. However, this causes more problems, and those that would be early are often two hours early and have nothing to do but get in everyone's way.

I have found myself in other disputes, not always involving the bride, groom, or family. I now believe it goes with the territory. I've had to jump in between two catering staff disputing over who was in charge of this table, who was pouring, wine, and who was clearing. Two staff one night literally went at it in front of guests over a simple priority of who was taking care of the family's table. I had to jump in and say, "This is not the place, ladies. Take it to the kitchen."

One dispute was with a church coordinator. Most churches have their own wedding coordinators, and we let them do their job and stay out of the rehearsal and wedding unless they want or need our help. I have a good relationship with most of these churches and work with the coordinator to get the bridal party down the aisle. This one church coordinator made it clear that this was her turf and no help or suggestions would be tolerated. In fact, she told me this when I showed up with the photographer for the rehearsal. The photographer and I were to sit in the back pew and keep our mouths shut. At one point during the rehearsal she told the bride to sit on one side and the groom on the other side of the altar until it was time for them to approach the priest for their vows. The bride asked if she could sit with the groom since she was nervous and would feel more comfortable if she could be with him.

The coordinator said, "No, this is the way we do it in this church." She was so stern that the bride started to cry. This was not the way the couple had planned this joyous time of their lives. When the groom asked if they could please sit together, coordinator said again, "This is the way we do it, this is the way God wants it, and this is the way it will be." Okay, now the bride is really sobbing. The bride's mom came to the photographer and I and asked us to please do something.

The photographer and I approached dragon lady and asked her to be kinder. What difference did it make if they sat together before they joined the priest at the altar? We didn't think the priest would mind, and we were sure God wouldn't mind. She huffed and puffed and finally let them sit together but told the photographer and I to sit down and shut up.

Several months later I got a call from a friend that had just been asked to take over at this same church as the coordinator and since she had not done this before, asked for some suggestions and tips. Apparently dragon lady had had so many complaints, she was asked to leave the church. I would be glad to help this new coordinator and friend and was so relieved the other coordinator was gone. Why can't everyone be nice, especially in God's house?

Occasionally, I have gone head to head with other ministers or officiants. My goodness, Darlene, have you no respect for the clergy? When I say ministers or officiants, some of these have been family or friends that may not be familiar with the venue. One insistent friend/minister requested such an odd set up that I had to intervene. Nicely, I assure you. The minister wanted to stand in between the couple and the guests. The guests would be facing the bride and groom, but the minister's back would be in the way. He wanted exactly four feet between the couple and himself. This would also push the guest seating back. The minister wanted ample space to walk around during the ceremony. It was important for the guests to see and hear him. I tried to explain that this was not a church service and he was not at the pulpit. The photographer and guests would like to see the bride and groom. "I'm sorry, sir, but this is not about you." I talked to the bride's parents and they agreed, but he was a distant relative of the groom. Okay, I may have to lose this one.

The next day at the wedding I explained this to the photographer, and he said, "No way, he's not going to steal the thunder from our couple. I'm being paid to get photos of the couple, not him!" The photographer went to the minister and explained in great detail about lighting, logistics, angles, etc. until the minister was so confused that he agreed to stay in one place and not in front of the bride and groom. At the end I was gracious and told the minister how much I liked his ceremony. I even got a hug from him. Sometimes, we do win.

A few years ago we had a bride that was not really difficult but indecisive. She had a large guest count at an elegant venue in town. The ceremony would be outside, cocktail hour on a covered patio, and dinner inside. The guest count was close to one hundred and seventy-five, so I brought in two of my best and most experienced coordinators. I had worked with the florist and the venue before, but the photographer and DJ were new to me and had been hired by the bride and groom. It was predicted to be a very hot day, so extra coolers had been set up as well as numerous shade umbrellas.

I was scheduled to do the rehearsal since both of my girls were scheduled at another event. I showed up at the venue twenty minutes before the scheduled five o'clock rehearsal. The groom and the bridal party were on time and brought me boxes of place cards, programs, favors, and décor that they wanted on the tables for display. An hour passed and still the bride had not shown up. The maid of honor, who was also the bride's sister, told me that the bride had called and that she would be another hour since the traffic was bad. I spoke with the venue, and they had another event scheduled for that night. We either do the rehearsal now or not at all.

I ran the rehearsal quickly with the Bridal party, where to stand, how to stand, when to enter, and how to exit. The rehearsal went smoothly, and I stopped by the rehearsal dinner site to make sure that they were set and let them know that the bridal party would be late for the rehearsal dinner.

I found out the next morning that the bride was an hour late for the rehearsal dinner.

On the wedding day, I stopped by the venue early to check on the set up. Both of my girls were on site and in charge of the wedding for the day. They were doing a great job with the set up. They had twenty-five dining tables to deal with, put out place cards, flavors, table numbers, etc. The florist had brought in an assistant since she had a big set up. When I left to do another event, my girls were ready to go.

I found out later that night from my lead coordinator that the bride had arrived an hour late for photos, which put the whole schedule behind. When it was time for the ceremony to start, my girls lined up the bridal party and signaled the DJ and photographer that they were ready to roll. The bride was reminded that they were ready and told to please line up with her dad. She said, "I'm not ready—it's too hot. I need to sit down for a bit."

So the girls asked the DJ to hold off, play more prelude music, and they would signal when the bride was ready. The guests are sweating it out in the heat, and the DJ said, "If she doesn't walk in five minutes, I'm walking out."

So my girls went back to the bride and told her it was now or never. The bride again said, "But I'm not ready. I need to check my make-up again."

God bless my gal, she can be tough, and she told the bride, "You are walking now. Stand up and let's go. You look great, but you cannot keep your guests sitting in the sun." The Bride did walk and the wedding went off without a hitch. I got a call at the end of the night from my gals; all had gone well, but the bride had to be led, pushed, and pulled throughout the night. The bride did give them a big hug at the end of the night and thanked them for being firm with her. She mentioned that at times she could be indecisive. Really? Sometimes in this business you have to be tough.

Some things I would list under tacky but not bad behavior. One such couple had a beautiful wedding at a private home in the hills above the

Valley. All had gone well, the ceremony, food, the photography, and it was a lovely, balmy night. Just when the guests were getting ready to depart and say goodnight to the bride and groom, the couple asked me to pass around a basket and ask the guests to chip in for their honeymoon. It seems that they were a few thousand short for their scheduled trip. This was the last thing that I wanted to do. The guests looked shocked when I approached, and they were as uncomfortable as I was. A few guests put in a dollar or two, but many just ignored me and the basket. I feel the same way about money dances, unless it's cultural or a family custom. I think its tacky and basically begging for money. If a couple has a tight budget, as most couples do, I suggest putting together a list of how much you want to spend for each vendor, photographer, florist, music, cake, coordinator, etc. Please use discretion with your choices. Maybe have a smaller guest list. Instead of two hundred, maybe invite one hundred. If you can't afford a full sit down meal, think about heavy appetizers and drinks at an appropriate time of the day, but please make sure that your guests know that its appetizers not dinner. Simplify your décor and maybe use more candles and greenery and fewer flowers. Instead of a large cake, think desserts or cupcakes. Have a smaller bridal party. Pick a fun family restaurant or pizza parlor for the rehearsal dinner instead of a fancy, high-end restaurant. Your rehearsal dinner should not compete with the wedding meal. Let your vendors know up front how much you want to spend and most are more than glad to help you stay within that budget. Jim and I often put together a budget for our couples so there are no surprises.

This reminds me of another night that I can say was tacky. The couple had picked a beautiful winery up in the hills for their venue. They were going to serve wine and heavy appetizers after the six o'clock ceremony. Dancing would continue until ten o'clock. I had told the bride and groom to please put on the invitation appetizers only, so guests would not expect dinner. Apparently our couple did not put this on the invitation and did not let the guests know that dinner would not be served.

After the ceremony and during the cocktail hour, the caterers came to me and let me know that the guests were not eating the appetizers. They had nibbled on them but had not taken full advantage of all the tasty choices. The guests were waiting to be invited into dinner, and that wasn't going to happen. I asked the DJ to announce for the guests to please enjoy the appetizers since there was not to be a sit down dinner. There were plenty of appetizers, enjoy, etc.

Within thirty minutes, most of the guests had left to find a nearby restaurant for a proper dinner. Most had traveled from out of state for this wonderful wedding and wanted to enjoy our Valley's wonderful cuisine. When it became obvious this experience was not going to happen, they left. The bride and groom were puzzled and upset with their guest's swift departure. The caterers wrapped up all the leftover appetizers for the couple to take with them. "How did this happen?" they asked.

"I'm so sorry but I reminded you to let your guests know that you were serving appetizers, not dinner." When you host a five-hour event, your guests assume that a meal will be served. That assumption should be correct.

Another couple asked if they could have two hundred guests to the church for the ceremony only, and invite only fifty to the reception dinner. They would get more gifts and have to feed less people. "No, I'm sorry, but that's tacky." If you can't afford to feed them, then don't invite them. Or pick a time in the middle of the morning or middle of the afternoon where you can get away with appetizers and drinks. Make sure your guests are aware of this by stating it clearly on the invitation. Most weddings that we do are destination weddings, and your guests are traveling from all over the country or even the world and are already spend a great deal of money on travel, hotels, etc. and a nice gift. So why ask them to pay for your honeymoon or not provide them with a nice meal? A wedding and reception can be done tastefully on a budget by using imagination and consideration for your guests.

Chapter 20:

Disasters, Fires, Earthquakes, and Pandemics

At 3:20AM ON AUGUST 24, 2014, our small valley experienced a magnitude 6.0 earthquake. Jim and I had done a wedding the night before, and we had been asleep for about forty-five minutes when this terrible earthquake hit. It sounded like a train roaring through the house and the lights immediately went out. In my exhaustion, I knew something terrible was happening but wasn't sure what. The bed was shaking and with the terrible noise. It was like a monster was in the house. Jim said, "Earthquake...don't move."

There is...was...a huge mirror over our bed, and I knew I had to get under a door frame. That's what I heard you're supposed to do. That or get under a table. I had to get up, and Jim was holding me down. We moved to the middle of the bed where hopefully we would not be hit by the mirror. After seconds or minutes (I'm not sure) it stopped. I tried to turn on a light, but they were out. I found my cell phone and got enough light to find matches in the nightstand and a candle in the bathroom. Jim went downstairs to check the damage and the cat. He yelled back up to me, "Don't come down! There's glass everywhere!"

I tried calling my two daughters that live in Napa, and the phones weren't working. I then called my younger daughter that lives on the Central Coast some five hours away, told her what was happening, and turned on the radio to find out what had happened. She told me to check on her eighty-nine year old grandmother who lives in Napa. She's my ex-mother in law and a wonderful lady. Jim and I got dressed the best we could in the dark, ignored the mess around us, and headed for Grandmother's house. When we got to Grandmother's house, she was on the front lawn with her neighbors, my son in law, and middle daughter. They knew they had to check on grandma first. No one was hurt, but lots of damage and tears.

By five o'clock in the morning, Jim and I headed back home. All the stoplights were out so we had to drive carefully. We were scheduled to do a small elopement ceremony at eleven o'clock at a local winery, and then a bigger wedding that night at another winery where we had to be on site for set up at two in the afternoon. We couldn't call or text any of the vendors or the couples, so we just assumed we were going forward with the weddings and would show up as planned. We didn't know if there was damage to the wineries or to the other vendors. We laid down for maybe two hours but couldn't sleep, so we decided to check for damage now that we had sunlight.

We were lucky: we lost vases, china, wine glasses, always the good stuff, and a crack in the garage floor. Some pictures were off the wall but overall, we were okay. We headed for the first winery at ten o'clock to see if the smaller elopement would take place. The winery up Valley had not sustained as much damage. Some broken bottles in the gift shop but very little damage. Some of our local wineries suffered major damage with broken and overturned barrels and wine everywhere. It was catastrophic for these wineries.

We still didn't have light, but the winery had a generator. The ceremony was outside, so we were good to go. The florist was there delivering flowers for the small wedding, and then they would be doing the bigger wedding with us that night. The florist had not come out as well as we did. They had breakage at the shop, vases, etc. Our friend and fellow florist at that time owned a fish store with his partner. He had been at the store all morning with volunteers trying to save the fish. Unfortunately, they lost them all. The tanks had broken and the fish were on the floor with no way to save them. They closed the business after the earthquake and lost everything. Yet, here he was setting up for a wedding. A wedding is like a Broadway show; you have to carry on.

I was almost hoping that one of the weddings would cancel. I was exhausted. I had glass all over the floor at home and the cat locked up in one room with food and a litter box so she wouldn't get cut. As it happened, of course, no one cancelled. The couple for the morning wedding that been staying up Valley had felt it but thought it was exciting. This was their first earthquake since they had come from the East Coast.

We took a quick lunch break and then set up for the second wedding. The other couple and guests had felt the earthquake also, but other than being terrified were thrilled that the winery was okay and that the wedding could proceed. And proceed we did. Sometimes after a disaster or tragedy, people are so glad to have survived that the joy is magnified. All went well, no matter what the vendors had suffered, and everyone put on a good face. I was so glad to get to bed that night; we finally had electricity, and I was too tired to even care about aftershocks. Some homes didn't have power for days. My middle daughter and mother in law didn't get power back for three days. They suffered much more damage with broken toilets, flooding, and fireplaces down. This was the biggest earthquake I have ever been through and, God willing, the last one of that size. Some of our buildings in town are still closed down and chained off.

Our couple that had their wedding the Saturday night before the earthquake called on Monday to tell us not only had they literally been thrown out of bed at the local hotel, but that the windows in their rental car had broken and a looter broke into locked the car and stole the wedding gifts that they had left in the car. They'll never forget their wedding weekend.

The next traumatic event was the fires of October 8, 2017. We had been doing a wedding at an up Valley winery. The evening was ending, dancing winding down, and the bride and groom were saying goodnight to their guests. My DJ went out to his van to start loading out when he noticed that the hills behind the winery were bright red with fire. He immediately came back in and told Jim and I that there was a bad fire and that we needed to be careful driving home.

"It looks like the whole valley is going up," he said. We said goodnight to the bride and groom and left the winery shortly after midnight. As we were driving back home, a drive of twenty minutes or so, the car was rocking from the wind, and I was afraid that the trees along the highway would blow over on the car. The hills on both sides were flaming balls of red and you could see the ash flying through the air. I have to admit I was terrified.

Jim and I drove by our oldest daughter's house since they live in the country not far from the hills that were on fire. Our son in law was hosing down the roof, but he was determined they were not going to evacuate. I got our middle Daughter on the phone, and since she lives in town, she was fine. We turned on the news, and everything we heard was bad. Homes were being evacuated and some people were barely getting out alive. Some were not getting out. That weekend had been a big golf tournament at one of our big private country clubs, and the some of the celebrities were still at the club or were just leaving.

The fire must have started around ten o'clock, but because it was so windy the fire spread very quickly. Friends of ours that live at this club barely got out with the clothes on their back. They had just gotten to sleep when the fire hit with no warning. They were able to get one car out of the garage and literally drove across the course to get out and away from the fire. They lost everything: their home, clothes, and their sweet cat. Others that lived at this golf club drove through sand traps and over the grassy greens to get out safely. Our valley had never seen a fire like this before.

We finally drove home to a house with no electricity and the smell of smoke strong and acrid in the air. We were scheduled to do a wedding on

Monday at the same winery. Weddings are not unusual in the Valley for Mondays, Thursdays, Fridays, and most weekends. The pricing at the different venues can be less for the weekdays. We went to bed not knowing if we had a wedding the next day or not.

At seven o'clock Monday morning we were awoken by a pounding on our front door. Okay, what now? Are we being evacuated even though we live in town? Our early visitor was one of my favorite florists to check on us. We had not answered our phones, and he was worried about us. We had no power, and our cell phones were still downstairs. Our friend and florist was scheduled to do the wedding with us that day. "So are we doing the wedding or not? Is the winery even still standing?" he asked. Since none of us knew and we couldn't get in touch with the winery, we decided to have a quick breakfast and drive up there and check out the situation. We wore our usual black wedding clothes in case the wedding was still on.

When we got to the winery we were told that the Monday wedding would continue with restrictions. We met with the winery president and he had spoken to the bride and groom. They would be allowed to do the ceremony on the lawn with the cocktail hour on the back patio, and then dinner and dancing in the courtyard outside. Dancing would have to end by nine o'clock. The winery had lost all power, so everything had to be done outside. The menu would be adjusted to compensate for the loss of the oven. The guests were already in town after traveling from all over the country, so the couple felt like they had to go through with the wedding. We had never done this set up before for outside, and the room diagram Jim had done no longer applied. Well, plans are made to be changed, so we took the diagram, made some adjustments, and put the tables up in the limited space that was allowed. The couple had also hired a band, so they would have to be set up on a higher level with maybe a twelve-foot space left for dancing. The ceremony would take place at half past four on the lawn, with a shortened cocktail hour.

Some, if not most, of the catering staff were not there to help with the set up. Either they couldn't get there due to the fires, or they were home watching over their own homes. Everyone pitched in: the president of the winery, and his wife, the vice president, the chef and his wife, Jim and I, and our favorite florist. We set up tables, dropped linens, and put chairs on the lawn. Glassware was placed and the florist put out the centerpieces. The kitchen had to make do with some lanterns and flashlights. They used string lighting to form an aisle from the kitchen through the dark barrel room out to the courtyard. This was the only illumination the server would have to get the food outside. The generator would last until maybe nine o'clock if we were lucky. I would say that we had less than half the staff needed for the bar and meal service, but you deal with it the best you can. The couple and their families were wonderful and willing to go along with whatever the winery suggested. I penciled in the changes to my timeline to adjust to the shorter evening.

Guests arrived and were welcomed with sparkling wine. I should mention that the skies were dark with smoke and ash was falling everywhere. Jim had the presence of mind to go to Home Depot in the morning to buy masks for the staff and for the two of us. We covered the glassware with pieces of paper to keep the ash from falling in the glasses. The ceremony went well, as did the cocktail hour. The few servers that were working put on a brave face. I noticed a few of the servers crying because they didn't know if they would have a house to go home to or if their family was safe.

Guests were invited to be seated in the lower courtyard area and wine was poured as guests were seated. The bride and groom were announced in by the band and did their first dance in the small area we had allowed for dancing. Their steps had been modified to fit this tighter space. Dinner service started with the revised menu. The inside barrel room was dark black except for the string lights making a path to the kitchen and into the courtyard. The bar staff had set up a table just inside the door with candles to hold the wine bottles for dinner service. I don't know how the staff could see in the darkened room; I had a terrible time just trying to get to the kitchen with questions or changes.

I could not keep my mask on and make announcement, so I took it off and tried to take small breaths. I quickly realized that didn't help, but I had to be able to speak to the band and the guests. The guests were very kind and there were very few complaints. One lady had a ten-year-old child with her and asked why the child was not getting her pizza. I explained that we had no power for the oven, and the child could have extra pasta. But Mom said, "She doesn't like pasta and she wants her pizza."

I tried to explain nicely, "The hills are burning around us, the staff is in tears, and I'm sorry, but your child will just have to eat pasta. Your child can even have my share of pasta, because most of the vendors don't have time to eat or have chosen not to eat."

Dancing began and was tight in space, but some tables were pushed back and the guests made do and had a good time. Wine was replenished and again covered with paper. Toasts had been short and some prayerful. The band offered to stay until ten o'clock, but the winery president told them that the battery for the outside lights would not last that long. The couple was fine with stopping at nine. What a story guests could tell about their exciting night in the Napa Valley in the middle of the fires.

The cake was cut and a thank you toast was by done by the couple. A friend had made the cake and asked me to box up the remaining cake, which I am always glad to do. The chef's wife and I wrapped it the best we could in cellophane wrap, but we did not have a box for it and the friend had not brought a box. When I handed her the cake, she asked me if I could please put it in a box. At this point I'd had it and told her we couldn't find a box in the dark. Normally the cake provider brings a box. If she would like to wait fifteen minutes or so, I would be glad to dig around in the dark back room with a flashlight and look for a wine box or something, "but in case you haven't noticed, we are dealing with a dire situation and this is not a normal night."

"Oh my gosh," she said, "You're right. How selfish, I'm not even thinking about how awful this situation is for everyone. Please forgive me."

Just before nine the band announced that they had just heard on the radio that the next town up, Calistoga, twenty minutes away was being evacuated, and our town could be next. That was the end of that; guests said goodnight to the bride and groom and left the winery. Jim and I helped the bride and groom pack up their gifts and belongings and load up their car. The catering staff and winery personnel stacked up plates, wine glasses, and linens, and just stacked them inside the darkened barrel room. There was no thought of washing dishes or racking glasses; we just had to get out of there. Jim and I headed home to make sure that we still had a home. Our house is in town, so we were fine. The power was off and on. We had a glass of wine and went to bed. No dinner…we were just too tired.

∞

The next day we had to deal with the three weddings that we had coming up in the next two weeks. Would the venues, most of them up Valley, have power and allow these weddings? Would the air even be safe for those two weekends? The air was terrible and the skies dark gray. The news was asking everyone to stay inside due to poor air. Home Depot and other stores were running out of masks.

Our brides started calling first thing Tuesday morning, asking us to check on their venue and what we were going to do. Jim and I spent all day calling their respective venues, and it was concluded that most would not be able to be open the following weekend. Many still did not have power, and the air quality was too bad to do an outside event. The idea would be to move the wedding to an area where there were no fires, the Bay Area or Easy Bay. Jim and I would make inquiries and so would our couples.

By Wednesday we had found backup locations for our Saturday and Sunday wedding. A small winery in the East Bay would handle the Saturday wedding, and a hotel in the San Francisco area would handle the Sunday wedding. It's amazing what you can accomplish in twenty-four hours when you have to. It took a year to put each of these weddings together, and it took less than two days to move them.

The small winery and their staff were great to work with. They would provide the catering, and we would bring our vendors with us. Our DJ, photographer, florist, and cake provider were willing to travel with us to the new venues. The florist actually carried the wedding cake down in his van. These guys are still my heroes.

Jim and I went down early for the rehearsal on Friday so we could redo the diagram and go over the details with the winery personnel. They would do the setup of the tables and linens, provide the food, and I would handle the table diagram and put out the desserts since the bakery for the desserts was not able to do the setup. My timeline would fit the timing of the evening, and the ceremony would be held outside in front of the winery, cocktail hour on an upstairs patio, and dinner and dancing inside. The room was smaller than the other barrel room, so we had to adjust the tables and reduce the size of the dance floor, but overall it would work. Jim and I decided to stay in a local hotel so we could be on site early for the changes in set up. We were also avoiding the smoke at home.

The coordinator on site was great to work with and let me do my thing with our vendors but would step in to answer questions and give helpful suggestions. The night went better than we could have hoped and a local San Francisco TV station came out to record the ceremony for the news. I got back to the hotel that night to see our couple on the eleven o'clock news. They explained that the fires had not ruined their wedding but gave it a story that they would never forget.

The Sunday wedding at the hotel also went off without a hitch. On Sunday morning, we got a call from our next weekend's Saturday wedding, that they had until ten o'clock the next morning to decide if they wanted to hold their wedding at the up Valley resort. At this time the resort still had no power and did not know if they would in a week or not. Even if they did have power, the air quality might still be terrible. If the couple canceled by ten, they could get their money back. If they waited, they would lose their deposits. This couple lived in the Midwest, so they could not help look for other venues. They would go online and look for possibilities, but Jim and I would need to visit these sites.

Monday morning, armed with a list of four possible venues and wineries, Jim and I set out to find a workable venue. Ballrooms in hotels did not appeal to us or to our couple. There was a small winery in the

East Bay that could do smaller weddings. It was not as pretty as their original venue, but it did have possibilities. When we arrived at this new venue it looked very nice from the road and the parking lot. This might be the right choice. After we parked and walked around the back, we noticed that there was a large hole in the roof of this beautiful Victorian house. The hole had been covered by a tarp. The grounds were very pretty with lots of flowers and steps leading to different levels of the property.

We asked to speak with their winery event manager. She assured us that she did have this next Saturday available and would love to host this wedding. They could bring in a local caterer and we could bring in our own vendors. She explained that we could use all of the property except the house. Also, their tasting room as it had suffered a recent attic fire. That would explain the tarp on the roof. Yuck, more fire woes.

After walking the property, we determined that we could do the ceremony outside under some beautiful trees, the cocktail hour on an elevated patio, and then dinner and dancing in a separate building upstairs that opened one side to the mountains, with glass doors that could remain open all night. This room was smaller than my diagrams, but was workable. We could do the dining tables around the edges of the room and dancing in the middle.

Jim and I took pictures and sent them to the bride and groom. We went and had a quick lunch, and by the time we were finished, the bride and groom had called and approved the venue. We went back to the winery and had them e-mail a contract to the couple. While we drove home, I called the vendors, photographer, DJ, florist, and cake provider and told them the story. I asked if they'd be willing to drive two and a half hours to the new venue. Absolutely, they were game again. Yes, the florist would bring the cake again. When I got home I made the changes to the timeline and sent it to the new venue, the new caterer, and the other vendors. The caterer would bring in the linens, glassware, etc., and the venue had the tables and chairs. Jim drew up a new room diagram, and we were ready to roll.

The only snafu we had was on Thursday, the day before the rehearsal. When I went over the timeline on the phone with the winery event manager, she informed me that we could not have amplified music for the ceremony, only live music. I promised her that the DJ would keep the sound down, and the music was only for the precession and recession. He would not play for the cocktail hour. But she was firm on this. County ordinance— she had to follow the rules. Great, now I have one day to find a live musician and tell the bride and groom. I thought one musician is less costly, so a guitarist or a harpist could work.

I called a harpist that I have worked with us many times in the past. She lives in the Bay Area. She was free and would give us a discounted price since this was an emergency, and she's just a great lady. She would play for the ceremony and cocktail hour. I called the bride and groom, gave them the price, and they agreed.

Jim and I drove down to the winery on Friday morning planning to stay at the local Marriott Friday and Saturday night. When I checked into the hotel I was told that the groom had covered our bill, and the bride and groom and most of the guests were staying at this hotel. The hotel had given them group rates. Wow, what a nice couple. We did the rehearsal and our harpist came to scout out her set up. She had actually worked at this venue before.

The day of the wedding, we finished the setup of the ceremony site, double checked the dining area, and met the caterer. My vendors arrived, and the cake was just fine in the back of the florist's van. Our vendors had decided not to stay overnight even though the groom had offered. They didn't mind the long drive back. The ceremony was at five o'clock and was beautiful. The bride was amazing in her gown, and the groom stood up with his two small sons. This is one wedding when I did tear up. They were so good together, so obviously devoted to each other. We still get Christmas cards from them to this day, and e-mails checking on us.

Dinner was good, and the dancing fun, even though the dance floor was smaller, it all worked. Music had to stop at ten o'clock since that was also a county restriction, but by then I think everyone was ready to call it a night. After we cleaned up and the vendors left, Jim and I headed back to the hotel. When I peeked in the bar, I noticed that the party was still going. It had just moved from the winery to the hotel.

After two weeks of mostly being out of town, Jim and I were relieved that the smoke in the Valley was dissipating and the fires were almost out. The destruction and lives lost will never be forgotten, and you can still see the damage on the hills around the valley and the surrounding towns that had seen even more damage. The fires had jumped so quickly with the winds. Our friends are still not back in their home that had to be re-built. Some of those residents that lost their home decided not to rebuild and sold or tried to sell their lots. Fire insurance doubled in some cases. I have to admire the brave people in our valley and those surrounding towns that pulled together to help each other and save lives and animals. Horses were rescued and pulled by rope from car windows. Goats and sheep were put in the back of pickup trucks to free them from the fires. So many deer, wild animals, and pets were lost in that fire. Some lucky animals showed up weeks later to a home that no longer existed. But I guess all you can do is move on and pray this kind of destruction never happens again.

I should mention that since the fires our Valley and other surrounding areas have suffered black outs due to increased heat and the wind. The electrical companies, wary of another fire, will choose areas to have rolling blackouts when the weather or winds demand it. Most of the bigger venues and wineries have purchased generators so that we are literally never in the dark again during a wedding or event. Just last summer, Jim and I had a wedding, and we received notice that morning that our home would be without power. Great, we needed to shower, dress, and curl my hair and do make-up. I called a local hotel and asked if they could fit me in for one night so we would have a place to shower. I think half of the Valley had also thought of that and the hotels were quickly filling up.

We were able to get into a hotel a mile or two from us, and we went over checked in, showered, and got dressed. We said we would stay the night and check out the next morning. Napa has a two- night minimum, but the hotel staff knew us and were willing to make the exception. Jim and I did the wedding, came home after midnight, drove by our house and yes, the power was back on. So Jim went back to the hotel, got our stuff, and came home so we could be in our own bed with our kitty. Jim mentioned the next morning that we had just had the most expensive shower on record. We were in the hotel for one hour.

I thought we had seen it all and had done it all until March of 2020. We were all booked for a very busy season of weddings starting in April and going through November. Then COVID-19 was announced to the public in March and we started the shutdown. We have postponed over twenty-four wedding from this year to next year, 2021. Our couples have been amazing and kind and willing to do what they need to do to have their perfect day. Jim and I stay busy checking future dates and making sure that all their vendors are still available. We all want to keep the original team together if we can. We have moved some of these couple's weddings three times or more from April to August to October, and now to next June 2021.

Some of our couples have not seen or visited their wedding site and can't get here or can't get back to their home once they get here. I have a couple in Dubai that I have not yet met who can't come over to visit the site because they won't be allowed back into their country. A few of our couples have chosen to get married in a smaller ceremony or go to city hall, and then postpone the bigger wedding to next year.

One very nice couple has scheduled their wedding in Texas that is more open than California and allowing crowds, and they moved their wedding to their hometown in this state. I offered to help even though I don't know anyone in this state, but I was willing to try. I will not be going to this state, but I was able to find vendors for them; photographers, videographers, florist, musicians, bands, and the cake.

I found a lovely photographer in the state, and she gave me names of other vendors. We were able to put together a team. The bride's mother found the venue and the caterer, and I offered to share and update the timeline. That's what we've done. All the vendors have been wonderful, and I feel like I'm made new friends, especially this great photographer. Someday when this is over, I would like to go to Texas and meet this great gal.

Chapter 21:

Weddings Continue, I Hope

I PRAY THAT WHEN THIS HORRIBLE PANDEMIC IS OVER that we can continue to coordinate and officiate weddings. We now have thirty weddings for next year, 2021. These wonderful couples have been patient and deserve to have their perfect day.

Our vendors also need to get back to work; they miss their couples. Once you're in the wedding business, life is dull without it. It's like a drug; we need the highs, just not the lows. We are calling this our lost year.

I have kept in touch with most of the vendors, at least my favorites, and I know how they are spending their down time. We speak or text at least once a week. My favorite DJ, loves to fish and owns his own boat. He is now spending more time on his boat, and if I can't get in touch with him, I know he's fishing. He catches and releases. He also has a great partner and a sweet cat, and we text pictures back and forth of our cats, Kits and Cappuccino. Back in March when I couldn't find Clorox or paper towels, this great guy left both on my front porch.

One of our photographers is doing a lot of camping and mountain biking. He and his wife and young son just recently purchased a camper and are spending time finding new camping spots.

Another photographer is spending more time home with his children and playing more golf. Jim and I are also spending more time playing golf. It's an outdoor sport, and it's just the two of us.

I also talk to our favorite florist at least three times a week, and they are doing okay. Business is slower, but they have a great attitude and are spending more time with family. We're all a family, a team, and after all these years we care about each other and have each other's backs. The same goes for the venues that we have worked for years; the chefs, the event managers, the caterers, and all the others that makes sure that your wedding is perfect.

To all my wonderful couples that I have had over the years and the ones to come: thank you. Without you, my life would be boring. Easier maybe, but boring. There were days that I cried until I laughed and days that I laughed until I cried. As Bob Hope would say, "Thanks for the memories."

Photographs